THE ASHFORD BOOK OF SPINNING

THE
ASHFORD
BOOK OF
SPINNING

Anne Field

Benton Ross
Publishers Limited

Revised edition.
Published in 1988 by
BENTON ROSS PUBLISHERS LTD
2/46 Parkway Drive, Glenfield, Auckland 10

ISBN 0 908636 53 9

A Shoal Bay Press book.
Printed in Hong Kong through
Bookprint Consultants Ltd, Wellington.

CONTENTS

CHAPTER TEN: PATTERNS FOR HANDSPUN YARNS 84

Knitting abbreviations • Old world — new style tabard • Cables for the outdoor man • Sweater: beginner's luck • Daisy pullover • Handwoven scarf • A shawl for all occasions • Houndstooth tabard • Tomboy sweater • Handspun baby's booties and slippers • Children's stretch hat and mittens • Toddler's jacket, hat and mittens • Fleece lampshade • Novelty yarn lampshade • Handwoven tablemats • Felt egg • Handwoven jacket fabric • Felt bag • Circular hanging • Felt hanging.

ACKNOWLEDGMENTS

As a teacher of spinning, I have long felt the need for a practical book on spinning, therefore I accepted this commission with pleasure. Ashfords are more than a manufacturer of spinning wheels and looms; they also care about the end use of their products. This book is the result of that care, as it has been written in an effort to improve the skills and enjoyment of spinners. Ashfords make a comprehensive range of well-designed spinning wheels and equipment, and it is my hope that this book will promote full and skilful use of this range.

All the black and white photographs in this book were taken by my husband Edward, and his patient and painstaking work contributes much to a book such as this. Photographs are so necessary when describing and explaining spinning skills, and without his efforts and support, this book would never have been written. The colour plates were photographed by Lloyd Park.

I wish to thank another member of my family, my mother, Evelyn Bray, who checked and double-checked the script, and in the process learnt to spin.

I also owe my thanks to Bruce Tinnock, Senior Tutor in the Department of Wool Science at Lincoln College, who gave much advice and information for Chapter Two.

Many spinners have helped me in gathering information, notably: Margaret Stove who provided the description of spinning fine yarn on page 53 and a sample of fine yarn in photo **30**; Nola Fournier, Marie Murray, and Molly Duncan. Pam Baker, with her knowledge of angora and mohair spinning, was a mine of information. The angora samples in photo **51** were spun and knitted by her, and she spun the bulky yarn in photo **30**. Jill Dando helped with Chapters Eight and Nine on dyeing and felting. I owe them both special thanks. Particular thanks are also due to the family of the late Mrs Irene Firman of Geraldine, who gave me permission to use her superb samples of spun wool (see photo **14** and the fine mohair sample in photo **50**).

The colour plates in this book feature articles created by several different people who have all generously agreed to provide instructions for making them. My thanks go to Cindy Begg, Barbara Bevis, Jill Dando, Gwen Fox, Marian Gilbert, Robyn Henderson, Jill Hildyard, Mary Johnston, Evelyn O'Donnell, Joan Quigley, Irene van der Krogt and Wilma Wolfreys.

My students over the last twenty years have all unknowingly contributed to this book in many ways. Spinning is a social, not a solitary craft, and I have had a great deal of fun sharing this knowledge with other spinners.

Anne Field

INTRODUCTION

It is forty-five years since I made my first spinning wheel. In the small township of Rakaia and in a very small workshop I experienced the thrill of challenge, the frustrations of 'trial and error' and finally a sense of achievement in designing and making a spinning wheel. The first criterion was to make a simple wheel which would spin really well. Secondly, to be available in remote country areas, the wheel had to meet current postal regulations . . . that meant packing it in a flat parcel. Because of World War II, women were doing things they had never done before and if one of them was putting together a kitset spinning wheel, I was determined to make their job as easy as possible.

Then I went off to war too and my father supervised production.

When the war ended so did spinning. However by 1965 spinning had regained its popularity and because of past experience we were able to meet an unprecedented demand for more and better spinning wheels.

Over the years my concern has been to improve and develop new models, not only for the convenience of the spinner but also to streamline production in the factory. I could concentrate to the exclusion of all else. However I must be fair to my family and give credit for their help and encouragement — also the many spinners who are experts in their field.

Spinning is a craft which has been passed down by word of mouth and example and for this reason there are very few text books on the subject. It seemed to me there was a real need for Ashfords to produce a simple but comprehensive book of their own.

I was delighted when this commission was accepted by Anne Field, a well known local writer and craftsperson, who has combined her practical and tutoring skills to write this book.

I have truly enjoyed my long association with spinning wheels and am proud that this has been and continues to be a family business. I thank my wife Joy and daughters Gaynor and Heather for their personal help and interest. I am most indebted to our son Richard for his enthusiasm and managerial skills and know he will continue in the Ashford tradition when I retire.

My personal thanks also to the staff who make our spinning wheels and to the thousands of spinners in New Zealand and overseas who will, I believe, continue to find rewards and happiness in this fascinating hobby.

Walter B. Ashford

CHAPTER ONE

Learning to Spin

INTRODUCTION

While writing this book on spinning, I found myself constantly looking back to my own beginnings as a spinner 25 years ago. Recalling my struggles, excitement and tangles, has made me aware of your needs, and has helped me to write a book that is relevant to your needs now.

I can see myself, as a young mother, feeling isolated and alone all day in a strange city. One day I came upon two neighbours sitting under a tree spinning. I can still see, in my mind's eye, the whirring wheels, the fleece on the grass and the flashing rhythm of the treadles. It was so romantic and peaceful, all it needed was a violin playing, and lambs frisking, to complete the picture. Here was something my soul cried out for! Something peaceful and soothing I could do while rocking the cradle. As you can see, I also had idealistic notions about babies.

The first week of spinning is also indelibly etched on my mind, but for different reasons. I can remember the frustration as the wheel kept turning backwards, the wool either rushed in at great speed, or refused to go in at all, my back ached, I lost my temper, and the baby cried. However, I was not going to be beaten, I spun and knitted a pair of mittens, with yarn the consistency of hawser rope, and so heavy that it was an effort to lift a mittened hand. I was more proud of those peculiar mittens than I have been of some of my later and better work. I was hooked!

In trying to analyse that sense of accomplishment, the best answer seems to be in the 'completeness' of the task. I chose the fleece, spun the wool, and knitted the mittens all by myself. In this age of specialization we do very

few tasks from beginning to end. Hundreds of years ago we owned the sheep, spun their wool, and knitted or wove most of the clothing for our family. Was this only from necessity or did it also fulfil a basic need? Nowadays, it is certainly not a necessity but is it still a basic need?

If, through this book, you achieve that sense of accomplishment while mastering a relaxing, useful craft, I will have done my work. By passing on my skills, enthusiasm, and love of the craft, I continue that chain, begun 25 years ago under the trees.

Spinning is deceptive. It looks so easy, yet, as with all skills that require co-ordination of hand, eye and foot, it is a struggle until that magical moment when suddenly you have 'got' it. All the effort then becomes worthwhile. Learning to spin from a book cannot take the place of actual lessons, so try to augment this book with some practical lessons from a friendly spinner. However, this book will take you step-by-step through the spinning process, and the many photographs will help make up for the lack of practical lessons. This first chapter will introduce you to the basic spinning recipe and later chapters will add to this knowledge. It seems logical to explain other spinning techniques, types of wool and wheels later, when the basic steps have been mastered, and there is a foundation to build on.

The wheel used in this chapter is the Traditional Ashford wheel. If you have another type of wheel, refer to Appendix B for details of your particular wheel.

Apart from your hands, feet and eyes, there are two other ingredients in the spinning recipe. Firstly you need some fibre to spin, and secondly you need something to spin it on. In this chapter I will only cover the bare essentials of fibres and spinning wheels; just enough to start you spinning.

FIBRES

Wool is the easiest and most common fibre to spin, therefore it is a natural starting point. A really good fleece is essential for the beginner spinner. Do not accept any old fleece because you know you will only make a mess of it. Without going into the whys and wherefores, which will be covered later, I will give you two alternatives which will make learning to spin as easy as possible.

Photo 1 shows a lock from a suitable fleece (left). The staple length, that is the length of the fleece from the cut end to the tip, should be 10-15cm (4-6ins) long. As a beginner, you would be wise to choose a fleece from the crossbred range, which includes Romney, Perendale and Coopworth sheep, as these are some of the easiest to spin. The wool should be clean and greasy. This type of fleece can be bought from craft shops, woolstores or direct from the farmer. Test that this fleece will be easy to spin by pulling a lock from the fleece and, with your fingers, tease apart the tip, the uncut end of the lock. If the wool is reluctant to part, the fleece will need to be combed or carded. Instructions for this follow in Chapter Three, where flick carding, an easy method for a beginner, is described.

On the right is a piece of carded sliver. This is fleece wool that has been commercially carded, that is a process in which the fibre mass is opened and made even. Sometimes, before carding, the wool is scoured to remove the natural grease, but try to get greasy sliver, as this is easier to spin.

Before learning to spin on the wheel, try the following exercise which will explain the spinning process, familiarize you with the feel of the wool, and cover some of the terms used.

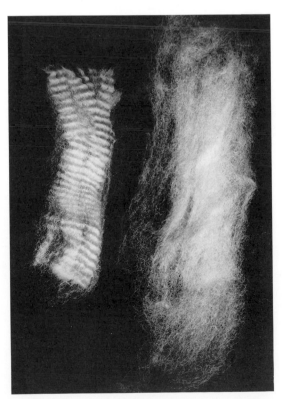

1 Lock of fleece and carded sliver

2a Take a lock of wool, and pull some fibres out with your right hand (left hand if you are left-handed).

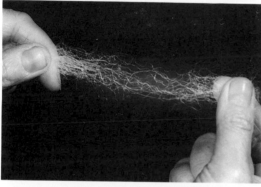

2b See how easily these fibres break.

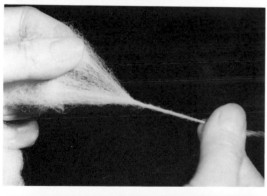

2c Pull out some more fibres, and twist them between the thumb and forefinger. Now try to break these twisted fibres. Note how the twisting has given the fibres much greater strength. This is the basic reason for spinning.

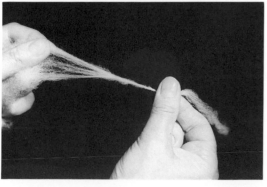

2d Continue to pull and twist fibres from the fibre mass. Rubbing the fibres down your thigh is a quick way to twist them. This yarn can be knitted into soft, airy garments without any further processing. However, it is soon evident that if you let the fibres go, they untwist and lose strength.

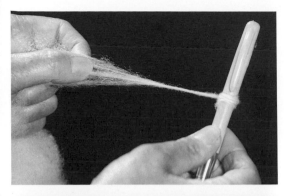

2e To hold the twist, wind the twisted fibres around the middle of a pen.

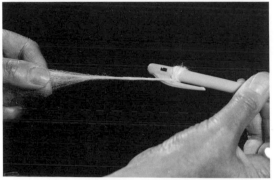

2f This is a slow process, and it becomes clear that if we can mechanically twist the fibres with one hand, while pulling out the fibre (drafting), with the other hand, the process is speeded up. Do this by anchoring the twisted fibres around the pen hook, twisting the pen with one hand while drafting with the other.

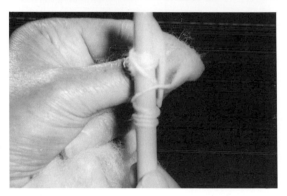

2g When the distance between the pen and the wool bundle becomes unmanageable, stop twisting, and wind the wool onto the pen shaft.

Practise the steps outlined above until you feel at home with them. If you have both fleece wool and sliver, try both types of wool, and use the easier one for your actual spinning.

The next few steps will show you how that first process in Stage I is related to the spinning wheel. Read through these steps a couple of times until the process is clear.

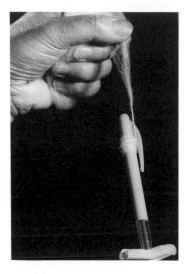 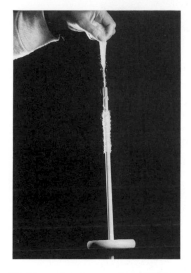

3a In order to quicken the twisting process I turn the pen on its end, add a weight on the unhooked end, and hey presto, I have a drop spindle.

The spindle was the earliest spinning device used, and is still quite common in some parts of the world.

3b To twist the wool, twirl the spindle rather like a top and the momentum given by the weight will twist the drafted fibres. This leaves both hands free for drafting, another step forward. A complete description of spindle spinning is given in Chapter 7.

However, I still have to stop and wind the twisted or spun fibres onto the shaft, although I can now spin a longer thread than before. This is where the spinning wheel comes in. Did you think I was never going to get there?

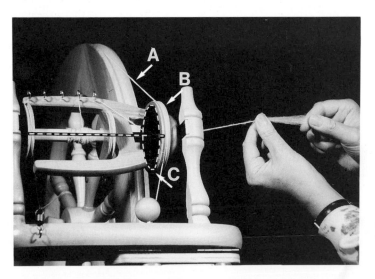

3c If I superimpose the spindle onto the spinning wheel, you can see how it fits together. Instead of my fingers twirling the spindle to set it in motion, my feet now put the twist in by treadling the drive wheel. A drive belt connects the wheel to the weight at the end of the spindle, which is now called the spindle whorl.

A Drive belt
B Spindle whorl
C Spindle

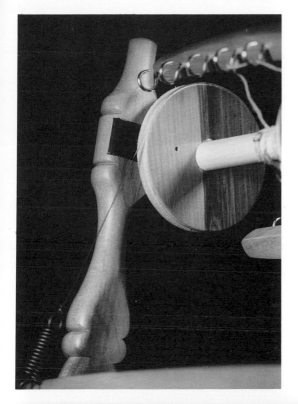

3d The twisting process is speeded up considerably, but I now need to get over the next barrier, that is, stopping to wind the spun fibres onto the shaft (now conveniently made into removable bobbins). The wheel does this for me, by slowing down the bobbin with a Scotch brake tensioning system. This brake is positioned at the opposite end of the bobbin from the whorl. When the brake is applied, the bobbin revolves slower than the spindle whorl, and the spun fibres are dragged onto the bobbin.

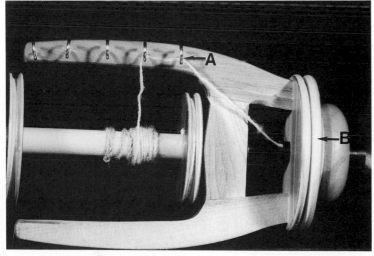

3e The spindle whorl, shaft and hooks, together are called the 'flyer', and the bobbin slips onto the shaft, thus allowing the bobbin to revolve at a different speed than the spindle whorl.

A Hooks
B Spindle whorl

The whole process will become clearer if you take the flyer and bobbin apart. Look at the connection between the bobbin and the brake band, and then the connection between the spindle whorl and the drive wheel.

4 Traditional Ashford wheel, with named parts

A Drive wheel
B Drive belt
C Spindle whorl
D Treadle
E Maiden bar

F Maiden uprights
G Flyer
H Drive belt tension knob
I Brake band tension knob
   (for Scotch tension)

J Crankshaft
K Lazy Kate
L Niddy noddy
M Bobbins

STAGE III: TENSION

Check that your wheel is correctly connected, with the drive belt running over the drive wheel, and over the spindle whorl. It should be firm but not tight. If it is necessary to tighten the drive belt, turn the drive belt tension knob to lift the maiden bar. Check that the brake band, the nylon cord, is over the larger end of the bobbin. It should also be firm, but not tight.

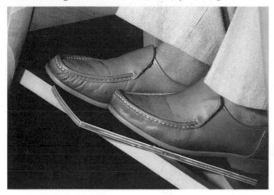

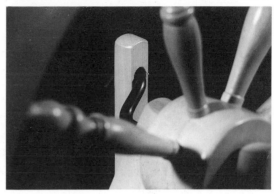

5a Practise treadling, using one or both feet on the treadle. Turn the wheel in a clockwise direction by giving the spokes a push with the right hand, and treadle as slowly as possible.

5b It is possible to start the wheel with no hands, by positioning the crank shaft at a 'one o'clock' position. This brings the treadle to its highest position, and it will automatically turn the wheel clock-wise with the first strong push of the feet.

5c Knot a 'leader', a piece of knitting wool about 3m (3yds) long, around the bobbin shaft, tying it very firmly with a couple of turns so it will not slip. Take the other end of the leader over the nearest distribution hook and thread it through the hole in the shaft and out through the orifice, using the threading hook supplied with the wheel. Let all the 3m (3yd) length pull through. Hold the leader near the orifice and treadle, letting the leader run lightly through the fingers. One of three things will happen:

1. The leader will disappear through the orifice at great speed. This means the tension on the brake band is too tight. Loosen it slightly by turning the brake band tension knob, allowing the nylon cord to slacken.

2. The leader will not pull on at all, but curl and twist in front of the orifice. **(5d)** Tighten the brake band by turning the brake band tension knob.

3. The leader will proceed gently through the orifice. This means the brake band tension is perfectly adjusted to allow the wool to wind on the bobbin. You would be very lucky to get this right the first time.

Setting the tension is perhaps the most important thing to learn when you are beginning to spin. Practise this step several times, until you can feel a slight pull on the wool as you treadle.

The amount of adjustment needed on the brake band tension knob is very small. Several minute adjustments are better than complete turns of the knob.

STAGE IV: SPINNING

The arrows in the photographs, indicate the direction in which the hands should be moving.

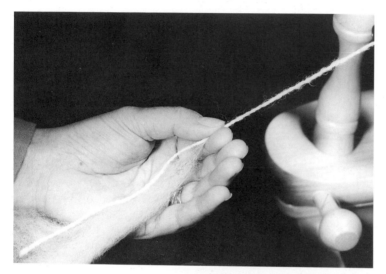

6a Wind the leader onto the bobbin until about 30cm (12in) is hanging from the orifice. If you are using fleece wool take about three or four locks and tease them apart with your fingers. With wool sliver teasing is not necessary. Hold the locks or a small amount of sliver in the palm of the left hand (if you are right-handed), with the thumb and fore-finger grasping a pulled-out portion of the wool and the end of the leader. The two ends should overlap about 5cm (2in) and be pinched together.

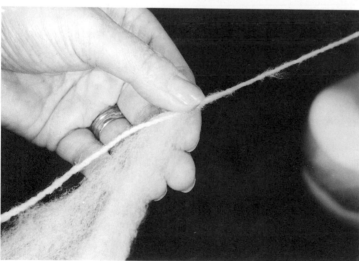

6b Start the wheel in a clockwise direction, and keep pinching the two ends together until the twist reaches the join. Maintain the pinch for a turn or two of the drive wheel to make the join firm.

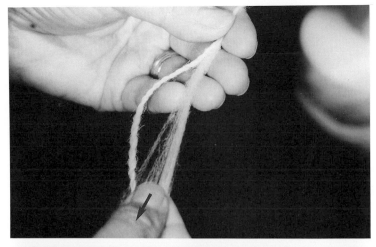

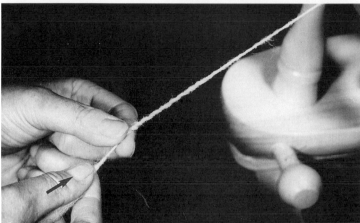

6c While this joining is taking place, take the right hand back to the loose fibres and draft them towards the body. The pinching fingers of the other hand give you a firm base to draft from.

6d Release the pinch of the thumb and forefinger of the left hand, to let the twist run into the drafted fibres and at the same time, bring the right hand up, allowing the drafted and now twisted fibres to run onto the bobbin. Both thumbs and forefingers should be about 3cm (1in) apart at this stage.

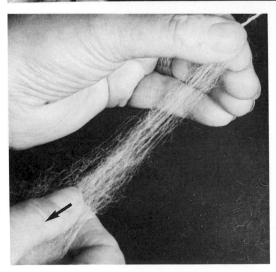

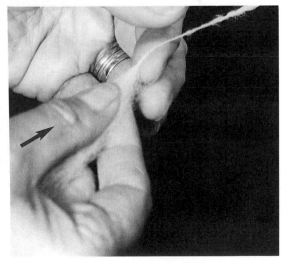

6e Pinch with the left hand again, and repeat the drafting-back movement with the right hand.

6f Release the pinch and bring both hands together.

These last two movements are the basis for all spinning, and it is this stage that needs constant practice, and is the most frustrating for the beginner. If you have mastered this technique within an hour of first sitting down at your wheel, congratulate yourself, as your co-ordination must put you in the genius level. Most ordinary mortals will need several hours, and some blood, sweat and tears, before they can reach this stage. It is difficult because you are attempting to co-ordinate three things, your feet, and your right and left hands, all doing different things and at different speeds. If you are one of those people who can rub your head while patting your stomach, this may help. Because this co-ordination is the key to spinning, you will suddenly find that you have 'got' it. This means that your hands and feet are working at the correct speed, in relation to each other.

An indication of correct spinning is that the wool between the front hand and the orifice should be twisted. Between the front and back hands the wool should be in a fan shape of drafted fibres, as in photo **6e**. These indicators will remain the same, although your hand positions will vary.

If you feel that the speed with which the wool is being pulled onto the bobbin is too fast or too slow, refer back to pages 17 and 18, parts 1, 2, 3 for guidance.

7 Concentrate on spinning with the correct amount of twist. To gauge this, pull about 10cm (4in) of wool from off the bobbin, and let it twist over and back on itself to form a plied thread. If little kinks and curls form, adjust the tension as in 2. If the yarn is loose and untwisted, adjust as in 1.

Do not worry about the lumps and bumps that form in the yarn at this stage, unless, of course, they are too large to go through the orifice. In this case break off the yarn and begin again as at photo **6b**. These lumps and bumps will disappear with practice.

If the yarn breaks, join it as in photo **6b**. When a small pile of yarn has built up in one place on the bobbin, move the yarn along to the next distribution hook. Frequent moving means the bobbin will fill evenly.

Practise these basic movements of spinning until you have two bobbins half full. By then you should feel comfortable with the movements. It would be too much to expect you at this stage to feel the rhythm and relaxation that are part of the joys of spinning, but this will come in time.

PLYING

The singles thread you have spun onto each bobbin can be used on its own, but for most purposes a 2-ply yarn is needed. Not only does this strengthen the yarn, but it also makes it more even. In a perfect thread, all the thick places on one strand would match with all the thin places on the other strand. Although this does happen sometimes, the beginner, with that lumpy, bumpy yarn, will wish it to happen more often.

When plying, the yarn from the two bobbins is twisted together in an anti-clockwise direction. This is the opposite direction to which the singles were spun. This unwinds some of the twist, causing the plied yarn to become softer and bulkier than the singles. The first two bobbins of singles were spun clockwise, and this is termed a **Z** spun yarn. The direction of the twist follows the centre stroke of the letter Z. To ply, the yarn must be spun as an **S** spun yarn.

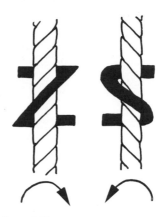

Fig. 1:1 S and Z spun yarn

The first stroke of each letter will help you remember which is the S or Z twist, as this is the way the wheel will be pushed to start.

Practise treadling in an S or anti-clockwise direction. Put the crank shaft in an '11 o'clock' position, and it will turn to the left automatically with the first push of the feet.

8a Put the bobbins onto the Lazy Kate, with the bigger ends on the same side. This prevents the yarn from tangling as it winds from the bobbins.

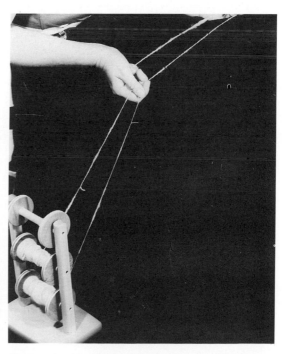

8b Put the Lazy Kate on the floor behind your right elbow.

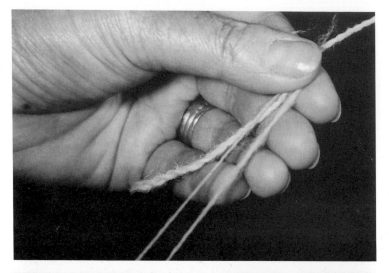

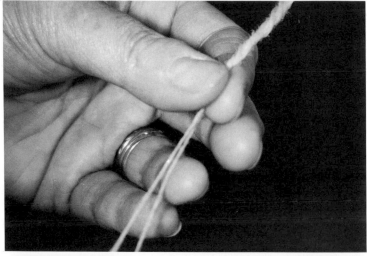

8c Take the two loose ends in your left hand, overlapping them about 7cm (3in) with the leader from the empty bobbin on the wheel.

8d Begin treadling anti-clockwise and pinch the leader and the two strands with the thumb and forefinger of the left hand until they twist together.

8e The right hand rests on your hip, remaining stationary for the entire plying process. Hold the two strands taut, separated by the fingers.

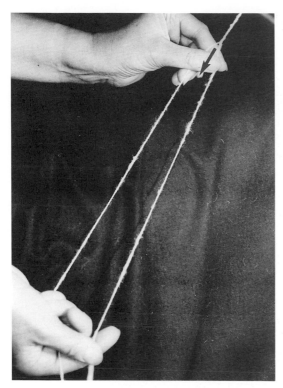

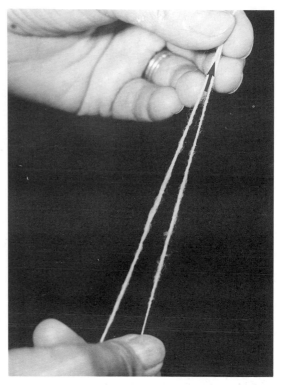

8f Release the pinch, and let the twist run back, supporting and accompanying the twist with the left hand, until the twist meets the back hand. The yarn should ply together just in front of the left hand.

8g Pinch with the left hand, and then propel the plied yarn into the orifice. These two movements (**8f, 8g**) will ensure even plying.

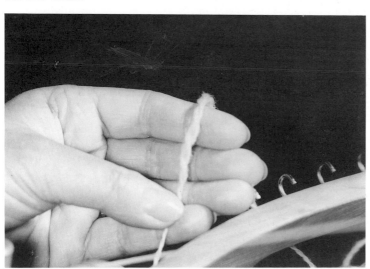

8h Test for the correct amount of twist in the plied yarn by pulling some of the yarn off the bobbin. It should be evenly twisted with no kinks or curls. The tension can be altered by turning the brake tension knob.

The bobbin will fill rapidly and the plied yarn should be moved along the distribution hooks regularly. As the bobbin fills, it becomes heavier. Tighten the tension to compensate for this.

SKEINING

When the bobbin is full of plied wool, loosen the brake band to allow the wool to be wound off onto the niddy noddy.

9a Stand over the wheel, take the loose end of yarn, and hold it against the upright of the niddy noddy with one hand.

9b Take the yarn in the other hand and wind it around the niddy noddy, following the arrows. The yarn goes over the upper cross-piece and under the lower cross-piece.

9c It is quicker to move the niddy noddy and keep the yarn supply stationary. It is this nodding movement that gave the skeiner its name.

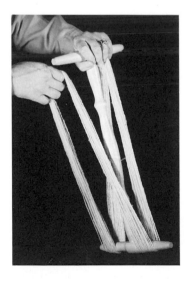

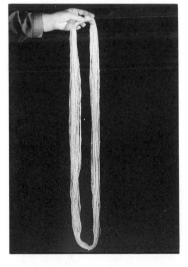

9d When the bobbin is empty, tie the skein loosely with both ends of the yarn and pull it off the niddy noddy.

9e Hold the skein at one end and let it hang loosely. If the skein hangs straight, the yarn is spun and plied with equal

amounts of twist in the spinning and plying.

If the skein twists in an S direction, there is too much twist in the spinning compared to the twist in the plying. If the skein twists in a Z direction, there is too much twist in the plying compared to the spinning. An unequal twist in either the spinning or the plying will cause knitted garments to angle to the left or right. The left-hand skein in photo **10** twists with a Z twist, therefore it has too much twist in the plying.

WASHING

All wool should be washed to set the twist. There are two methods of washing handspun wool.

First method
This leaves the wool clean but greasy, and is suitable for outdoor, semi-waterproof garments such as a fisherman's jersey. Soak the skeins in cold water for an hour or two. Change the water when it gets dirty, and keep soaking until the water becomes clear. Dirty wool may need three to four changes. Agitate the skeins occasionally, but do not rub the wool strands together.

Second method
This leaves the wool clean and almost grease-free, and is used when the water-proofing qualities of wool are not needed, as in a woman's lacy jersey. Soak the skeins in warm water for an hour or two. Transfer the skeins to a warm bath of soap suds, using well-dissolved soap powder, soap flakes or detergent, and soak. Change the water when necessary. Rinse in warm water.

Skeins washed by either method can be spun-dried in the spin cycle of the washing machine, to remove excess water. Do not tumble dry as this causes shrinkage and felting.

10 Hang the skeins on the clothes-line over a nylon stocking to dry, turning occasionally.

11 Roll the skein into a neat hank. Slip each end of the skein over each thumb, hold it taut, and twist. Slip one end loop through the other.

When the yarn is dry, examine it critically. Some common faults are shown in photo **12**.

12 Faults in spinning

A. A tight, thin singles is plied with a thick loose singles. This means each bobbin was spun at a different tension.
B. The yarn kinks and curls and feels harsh. This means the brake band tension was too loose in either the spinning or the plying.
C. The yarn is loose and fluffy and breaks easily. This is caused by too much tension on the brake band.
D. The yarn has thick places that are loose and soft, and thin places that are tight and over-twisted. This is caused by uneven spinning, that is, in the drafting process, uneven amounts of wool are pulled out. This is a common beginner's fault, and it disappears with practice.

Examine your finished product critically, and decide where it could be improved. This enables you to adjust your spinning, and ensures that the next skein will be better.

Do not be discouraged by the look of your first skeins, which will probably look very like **D** in photo **12**. When knitted, it is amazing how the lumps disappear, and you may even be complimented on the 'textured' look of your yarn. Use this first wool for small projects, such as hats and mittens. If you attempt large garments, your wool will improve with such rapidity that the front and back of your garment will look completely different.

Having reached this stage, it is now a case of practice, practice, practice. It is a good idea to spin 1-2kg (2-4lb) of wool, aiming at improving each skein. Fifteen minutes' practice every day will be more helpful than five hours once a week. Try using the right hand as the hand nearest to the orifice while spinning or plying. Some people, whether right or left-handed, find this easier.

The method of spinning (the short backward draft) described in this chapter is only one of many. Other methods, suitable when producing other types of yarn, will be described in later chapters. However, when you are learning to spin, it is best to become completely familiar with one method before graduating to others.

As you practise your spinning, try to develop the rhythm that is so much a part of spinning. This will help you to relax, and also enable you to use the techniques explained in Chapter Five. Try one drafting movement for one push of the treadle. This will probably be too fast for you at this stage, so try one draft for two pushes of the treadle. Counting out loud will help, even if it drives your family to distraction. When you find a comfortable draft and treadle rhythm, maintain this for an entire project.

The length of the draft, that is, the length of wool between your two hands, will depend on the staple length. If the staple length is 10cm (4in), the draft length should be the same. This draft length should also be the same for each project. Consistency of yarn will come when both the treadle count and draft length are uniform.

CHAPTER TWO

Wool

Classification • Breeds • Spinning with sliver • Choosing a fleece • Sorting a fleece • Storing a fleece • Washing fleeces • Dressing mixtures.

In this chapter, we will look at the raw material: wool. The wool trade uses terms that may be unfamiliar to spinners, so check the glossary at the end of this book for the meaning of new phrases and words. Wool classification varies from country to country and I have kept to the New Zealand terms with which I am familiar.

If you have the opportunity to attend classes or talks covering breed wools and their characteristics, do make the most of these. Many guilds and groups do run such courses, and they will give you the chance to study and handle the fleeces from different breeds of sheep — an invaluable experience.

Wool is the fibre grown by sheep, and it has two properties that make it the easiest fibre to spin. First, each fibre clings to the next. This is due to the outside layer of overlapping scales on each individual fibre. Secondly, wool has a natural grease, which acts as a lubricant while spinning.

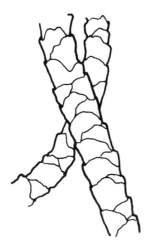

Fig. 2:1 Magnified wool fibre

There are over a hundred breeds of sheep in the world and each of these breeds has its own type of fleece. Not all these breeds produce wool suitable for spinning, but we should know the characteristics of the main breed wools which are suitable, and how to use them. It seems sensible to start with a fine, soft fleece, when the finished product is to be a fine, soft jersey, yet many spinners still choose a fleece at random. They then wonder why the finished article does not look as it should.

Wool can be classified into groups ranging from fine to strong (coarse) wools. The fineness of the wool can be described by either the micron estimation or measurement given to that type. This refers to the average fibre diameter, and is gradually replacing the quality number (or count) system of fineness estimation. The quality number is an estimate of spinning capacity, based on how many hanks of yarn can be spun from a given weight of top. With the increasing use of sophisticated equipment which can accurately measure fibre diameter, the quality number system is becoming less used. Microns refer directly to fibre diameter, hence the smaller the micron number, the finer the wool.

Appendix A lists and describes the main breed wools used in hand spinning in different parts of the world. Note how some breeds, e.g. Romney, can be placed in both the fine and medium class of the crossbred wools. The range of fineness of Romney wools is such that it extends beyond one class. The beginner spinner would be wise to choose fleeces from the fine/medium crossbred range as these have a good length and are easy to spin. These fleeces will have a staple length suitable for spinning, ranging from 100-150mm (4-6in), and a close crimp spacing.

A coarser wool will be less white in appearance, harsher in feel, and have wider crimp spacing. Yarns spun from it will also be comparatively harsh, less white in colour after scouring, and less elastic. Fleeces should therefore be chosen with care.

Crimp is the wave pattern in a wool staple, and it is this wave in the wool fibre which helps give it elasticity. The amount of twist inserted when spinning each breed wool should also vary (see Chapter Five page 51, twists per cm). A yarn spun from a very fine Merino wool should have a high twist, while that from a coarser Lincoln fleece should have very little twist. To assess this twist, look carefully at the crimp pattern. The spacing of twists in the yarn should match the spacing of crimp in the raw material.

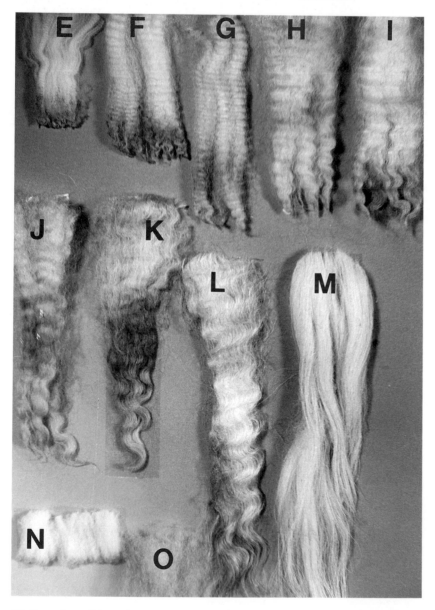

13 Samples of breed wools

E Merino
F Corriedale
G Perendale
H Romney
I Coopworth
J Border Leicester
K English Leicester
L Lincoln
M Drysdale
N Southdown
O Cheviot

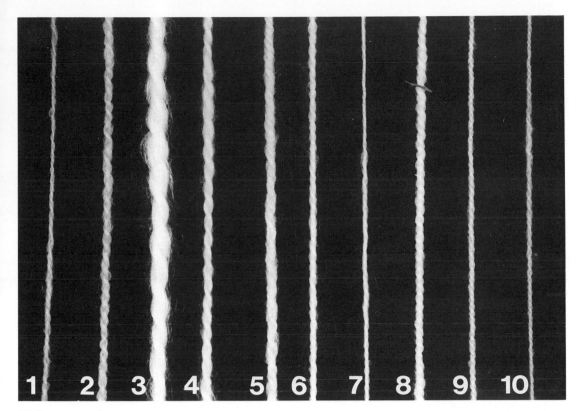

14 Spun samples:
1 South Suffolk, 2 Dorset Down, 3 Lincoln, 4 Border Leicester, 5 Coopworth (3 ply), 6 Romney, 7 Perendale, 8 Corriedale, 9 Polwarth, 10 Merino.

SPINNING WITH SLIVER

Sliver is the term for wool that has been commercially carded for the convenience of handspinners. This carded wool usually has most of the fibres arranged in one direction, which makes it easy to spin. This sliver looks similar to the carded fleece in photo **20i**, page 38. Sometimes the wool is scoured before carding to remove all the grease and dirt. In such cases a dressing mixture, such as that described at the end of this chapter, may be added to put back the grease content. Greasy sliver, resulting from carding of unscoured fleeces, can be spun as it is.

Sliver can be obtained in various forms. It may be purchased in large batts, similar to that shown in photo **20i**. Before spinning strip off a narrow piece of the batt to reduce it to a more manageable size. Sometimes the sliver is already reduced to narrow strips. If you hold a large amount in the hand while spinning, it will tangle.

Most sliver will have the breed wool it originated from indicated on the outside of the bag, i.e. 'Romney sliver', or it may be designated a class, such as 'fine cross-bred'. With this information, you will be able to make decisions based on the known quality, fineness and handle of the wool, using data given in Appendix A. It is more difficult to see the crimp pattern and breed characteristics in wool sliver, as the carding process modifies these, but there are advantages to using sliver, as opposed to fleece wool. Sliver is clean, with no wastage, and no sorting or washing is usually necessary.

CHOOSING A FLEECE

Once you have chosen the type of fleece that will best suit the finished article, look for the following points in a particular fleece.

Cleanliness
The fleece should be free of vegetable matter such as seeds, thistles, burrs or twigs. Avoid excessively dusty or dirty fleeces. Choose a fleece that does not have excessive entanglement of fibres, as these fleeces are difficult to card and spin.

Soundness
The fleece should not have a break along the staple length. A break is a tender part of the staple, caused by a reduction in feed intake resulting from sickness, drought, or other adverse conditions. Test for soundness by pulling and snapping a staple between the fingers of both hands. The staple should not break apart. Sheep shorn before lambing generally have sounder fleeces than those shorn after lambing.

Discolouration
This can be caused by many factors. Avoid all wool with stains, and yellow discolouration that will not wash out. Test the scourability of a fleece by washing a staple under cold running water. A good clean fleece will become white almost immediately. In black and coloured fleeces, it is sometimes difficult to see stains and discolouration.

SORTING A FLEECE

Before using or storing a fleece it should be sorted. Most fleeces will have already been skirted, that is, the inferior portions will have been removed at shearing. If the fleece is not spread out and sorted before spinning, the standard of spinning may vary, in accordance with variations in characteristics throughout the fleece. Spread the fleece out where there is plenty of room. Outside, where there is good lighting, is the best place. If the fleece has been handled a lot, it might be difficult to untangle, but try to keep the fleece as whole as possible. The tips of the staples should be uppermost.

A. Remove any heavy, greasy pieces from the edges of the fleece, or any edges which are slightly discoloured. Remove the matted, seedy neck portions if present. Separate the britch portion (from the lower thighs), if it is stronger or harsher than the remainder of the fleece. The best wool is normally found on the shoulder and sides.

B. Remove the centre back portion, if this wool is found to be mushy and tender. Exposure to the weather and rain will cause a portion of the yolk to be washed away from this part of the fleece, leaving the staple tips weak and brittle. This back wool can be used in felting.

C. With a black and coloured fleece, it is useful to sort it into dark and light portions before spinning. Black and coloured fleeces are often not of as high a standard for handcrafts as white wool. For over a hundred years breeders have been improving the characteristics of their white fleeces, but it is only relatively recently that coloured wool has been grown especially for handcrafts.

STORING A FLEECE

Fresh new wool, that has just been shorn, is a joy to spin, as it has a liveliness and oily texture that is gradually lost with storing. However, there are many times when fleeces must be stored. Do not buy too many fleeces at once, and keep storage to a minimum, to prevent deterioration. Store them in unbleached calico bags. Plastic bags are not recommended as condensation will form. Label the bag with the type of fleece and the date it was purchased.

Once I had forgotten about two fleeces I had stored for years and rediscovered them only to find that one housed a nest of mice, and the other a horde of bees!

WASHING FLEECES

Sometimes it is necessary to wash a fleece. This is usually done before dyeing as greasy wool will not dye satisfactorily, or before drum carding to prevent soiling of the carding cloth. However, a very dirty fleece may also need washing to make it pleasant to handle.

Wash small amounts at a time. Wool has a tendency to swell and grow in bulk when wet, and what began as a small, manageable bucketful soon becomes a huge pile of sodden fleece. When I wash fleeces I can almost guarantee a weather change. A warm, windy day becomes cold and wet the moment I put a fleece to soak.

Soak the wool in warm water, changing the water frequently. Then soak in a warm bath of soap suds, using soap powder, flakes, or detergent, again changing the water when necessary. Rinse well. Do not stir or rub the wet wool, as this will cause it to felt. Put the wool in pillow-cases or mesh bags, then remove the excess water in the spin cycle of the washing machine. Spread the wool over wire-netting laid over the clothes-line to dry, and turn frequently. Never use a tumble drier to dry wool, as this causes felting.

DRESSING MIXTURES

Washing will remove the natural grease from the wool and this should be replaced, after the dyeing/carding has been done, and before spinning. Apply the dressing the day before spinning, then wrap the fleece and store it in a warm place to allow the oil to penetrate. Do not leave the oil on the wool for too long, as it can become rancid. Use a fine spray applicator, which can be bought from a garden shop. Another method of applying the dressing, is to keep a bowl handy while spinning, and dip your fingers in it.

The following recipes for dressing mixtures are all suitable. Blend well.

A. 1 part olive oil and 1 part water.
B. 1 part neatsfoot oil and 1 part water.
C. 1 part neatsfoot oil, 100g washing soda, and 1 part water.
D. 1 part olive oil, 1 part water, and a quarter part of ammonia.

Some spinning shops supply a water-soluble oil, mixed with water to form an emulsion, as a spinning oil. These shops may aso supply a moth-proofing agency which can be added during washing.

CHAPTER THREE

Carding

Combing · Flick carding · Handcarding · Drumcarding · Blending.

Carding is the process in which the fibres are opened and spread more evenly in preparation for spinning. Not all fleeces need carding. A long-stapled, clean fleece, with no cotting or matting at the tips, may be easy to spin just as it is. Experiment with the wool, spinning some of it directly from the fleece. A good fleece will draft evenly with the same number of fibres in each draft. If this does not happen, the fleece will need some preparation first.

Different carding methods and equipment are used in the preparation of wool when spinning either worsted or woollen yarn. These techniques are described in Chapter Five.

15 Comb (top), flick carder (bottom), and handcarders.

COMBING

A metal comb can be used to comb and separate the tip of the staple. This method is suitable when the fleece needs very little preparation, or for worsted spinning. Place a piece of heavy material or leather on your lap.

16a Grasp a staple of wool firmly in the left hand, at the cut (butt) end, and hold it against the background material.

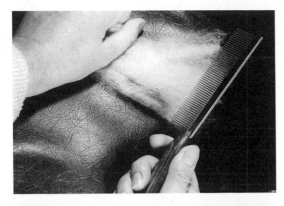

16b Hold the comb in the right hand, and sharply tap the comb into the tips of the staple. The movement is more a hitting than a combing action.

16c Continue until the wool is open and smooth. If necessary, turn the staple over to comb the other side.

FLICK CARDING

When heavier carding is needed, and also for worsted spinning, use a flick carder. This is a small wooden batten with metal teeth. Use it on a firm surface such as a piece of leather. If the flick carder is used on a hard surface, the metal teeth will become displaced. Grasp the wool staple in the left hand, at the butt end.

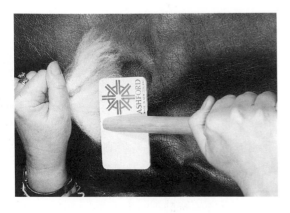

17 Flick the carder down onto the tips of the staple. Again, it is a hitting motion, not a combing one.

If most of the staple collects on the carder, you are not holding the wool firmly enough in the left hand, or you are combing the wool, rather than tapping it. The action should be a downwards wrist movement.

If necessary, turn the staple over to card the other side. Take care that the carder hits the wool, not your left hand, as this is a painful process rather akin to hitting yourself with a hedgehog.

HANDCARDING

Handcarders are mainly used to prepare wool for woollen spinning (see Chapter Five), or for very tangled or cotted fleeces. They are also useful for blending different fibres or colours together. Worsted spinning, as described in Chapter One, usually needs only combing or flick carding to prepare the fleece. For woollen spinning, however, the yarn is spun from a rolag which is a sausage-like roll of wool. The wool is carded, then rolled so the fibres are coiled around a central core of air.

Handcarders are large wooden battens, with metal teeth embedded in a leather backing.

18a Place one carder on your lap and fill the carder with staples of wool. Press the butt end of each staple into the metal teeth with the thumb of the left hand, while pulling on the staple with the other hand.

18b Brush the right carder lightly across the left carder several times.

18c This will transfer about half the wool onto the right carder.

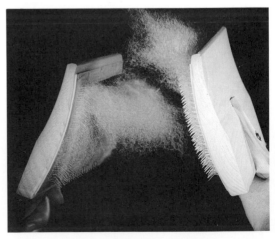

18d The carded wool is then stripped off both carders. Hold both the carders upright, and place the upper edges together.

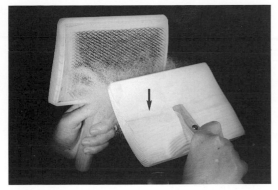

18e Pull the right carder down, stripping the wool off the left carder.

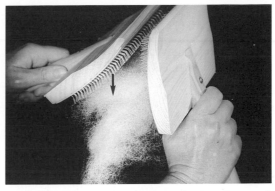

18f Pull the left carder down, stripping the wool off the right carder. Do not tangle or bend the wool in the process.

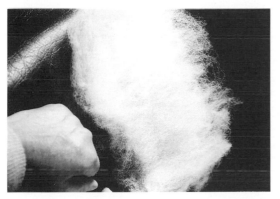

18g When carding is complete, place the loose mass of parallel fibres on your lap.

18h Roll the wool into a rolag.

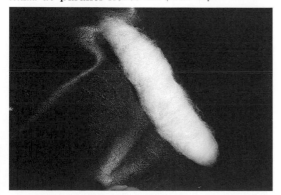

18i Finished rolag.

There are many methods of carding on hand carders, but the secret of all correct carding is to do small amounts of fleece wool at a time. If too much wool is placed on the carder only the top layer will be carded.

Check the mass of fibres after they have been removed from the carders. All the fibres should be parallel, with no short noils, clumps of wool, or extraneous matter in the wool.

DRUMCARDING

A drum carder is useful for carding large amounts of wool, or when woollen spinning. The carding cloth, with its metal teeth, is attached to a large and small roller, which rotate against each other when the handle is turned. The wool can be washed first (see Chapter Two) to prevent the grease and dirt soiling the carding cloth. However, the Ashford carder has a rubber backing, and washing is not essential. If the wool is washed a dressing mixture as described in Chapter Two should be added before spinning.

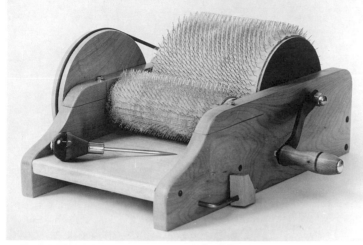

19 Drumcarder

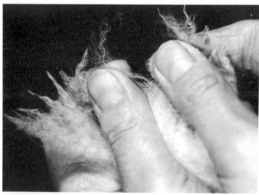

20a Tease the tips of the staple apart.

20b Place a few staples across the width of the feed tray.

20c Turn the handle away from you, to draw the staples under the small roller. Do not hold the fibres back as this tangles them around the small roller.

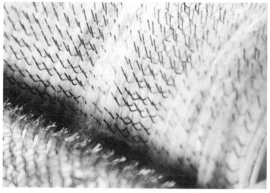

20d The fibres should wind onto the larger roller. Continue turning the handle until all the fibres lie smoothly on the large roller.

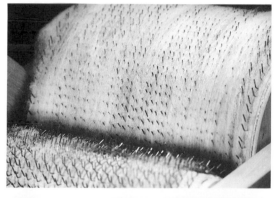

20e Continue the steps from **a-d** until the larger roller is evenly filled to the top of the teeth.

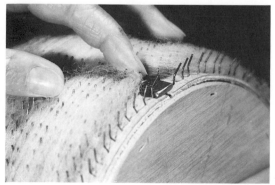

20f This layer of wool, the batt, is now removed. Rotate the rollers until the metal strip across the larger roller is uppermost.

20g Insert the metal awl under the batt at this point, and break the batt. Do not cut.

20h Rotate the handle towards you and peel off the batt. If the fibres are not parallel, a second carding may be necessary.

20i For worsted spinning, break the batt into length-wise strips before spinning.

20j For woollen spinning, the batt is broken into strips and rolled into rolags.

BLENDING

Drumcarders are ideal for blending dyed or coloured wools to ensure an even colour mix. They can also be used to blend two or more different types of fibres together, such as mohair and wool. When blending different fibres together choose compatible fleeces with similar properties. Card each colour or fibre separately, and then use one of the following methods.

A. Place a layer of one colour/fibre alternately with the other on the feed tray.

B. Place one colour/fibre on the left side of the feed tray, and the other colour/fibre on the right side. The colours/fibres can be reversed halfway through the process.

C. Short pieces of wool, which will form slubs during spinning, can be carded into the batt.

D. Short pieces of contrasting yarn, fed in at irregular intervals while carding, will add a random colour effect when spinning.

E. Other fibres can be added to the fleece wool, such as dog hair, alpaca, camel hair, or silk tops. With short fibres, the addition of longer, fleece wool stabilises the batt and makes it easier to spin.

CHAPTER FOUR

Wheels

How a spinning wheel works • Drive ratio • Scotch tension system • Double belt system • Advantages and disadvantages • Maintenance of wheels.

HOW A SPINNING WHEEL WORKS

In Chapter One I described the basic spinning system with enough detail to enable you to start spinning. However, now you have mastered the basics, it is time to learn the finer points of how your wheel works. This will enable you to get the most from your wheel, and to understand the differences between wheels.

To re-cap Chapter One, every spinning wheel has a drive belt connected to the flyer/bobbin unit. This belt causes the bobbin to revolve when the wheel is treadled. The bobbin must revolve at a different speed from the flyer, to enable the spun yarn to be wound onto the bobbin shaft.

DRIVE RATIO

On the Traditional wheel the drive belt is connected to the spindle whorl. When treadling, this connection causes the flyer to revolve.

21 Drive ratio on the Traditional wheel
A Circumference of drive wheel
B Circumference of spindle whorl.

The circumference of the drive wheel compared to the circumference of the spindle whorl is significant as this determines the number of times the flyer will revolve for one revolution of the drive wheel. On the Traditional wheel (Scotch tension), the flyer will turn 6.6 times to one turn of the drive wheel. This figure is known as the **drive ratio**, and it is this factor which determines the number of twists put into the spun yarn. The example above (the Traditional wheel) means that 6.6 twists are put into the yarn for one revolution of the drive wheel. If you feed 2.5cm (1in), of wool for this one revolution of treadle, 6.6 twists remain in this stated length. The greater the difference between the circumference of the drive wheel and the spindle whorl, the more twists per cm (in) are spun into the yarn.

It is necessary to know the drive ratio of your wheel. If you have a new wheel, the ratio is in the literature which comes with each wheel, and will be written thus: 6.6:1. If your wheel is not new, the ratio can be found in the following manner. Tie a piece of yarn to the flyer. Put the crank shaft at its highest position, turn the drive wheel slowly by hand, and count the times the flyer revolves for one revolution of the drive wheel.

Because the drive ratio determines the number of twists per cm (in), it also determines to some extent, the thickness of your spun yarn. A fine yarn should have more twists per cm (in) than a coarse yarn. An experienced spinner can manipulate the wheel and yarn while spinning, to allow some freedom with the drive ratio but it is better, particularly for the beginner, to use the wheel within its pre-set limits. For most medium yarns, a ratio of between 5-8:1 is usual. For fine spinning, the ratio can be as high as 15:1, and for thick, bulky wool, the ratio can be 2:1.

On the Traditional wheel, as with some of the other wheels, the ratio can be altered by moving the drive belt to the smaller whorl, at the front of the spindle whorl. This will give a ratio of 10.5:1, and is suitable for finer spinning.

When you change the drive belt from the larger to the smaller whorl, the belt will need tightening. Do this by turning the drive belt tension knob. The drive belt may also need re-knotting or splicing. This ability to change the drive ratio on a wheel is a refinement that allows much wider use of a single wheel.

There are two main systems of spinning, the Scotch tension system, and the double belt system. These systems differ at the point where the drive belt connects with the flyer/bobbin unit.

22 Adjusting the drive ratio to 10.5:1

SCOTCH TENSION SYSTEM

This spinning system has the drive belt connected to the spindle whorl. The drive belt should be of sufficient bulk to provide maximum traction, with no slippage, and it should be tied with a flat knot, or better still, spliced and oversewn. This prevents the belt from jerking every time the knot passes around the spindle whorl.

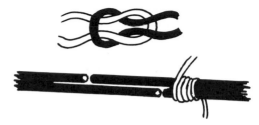

Fig. 4:1 Reef knot and splicing

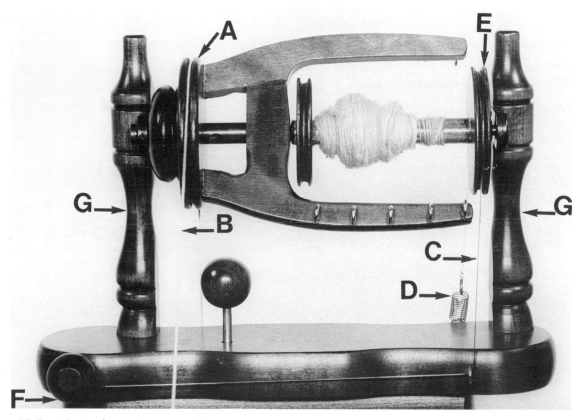

23 Scotch tension system:
A Spindle whorl, B drive belt, C Brake band, D Spring, E Bobbin groove, F Brake band tension knob, G Maiden uprights.

The brake band should be of smooth nylon, and is made of a different type of cord from the drive belt to allow some slippage while spinning. This slippage allows the spinner to hold back the yarn fractionally while spinning, to compensate for uneven places in the yarn, or to pick out seeds or other extraneous matter. The spring attached to the brake band gives the fine adjustment necessary when tightening or loosening the brake band. Remember that a tight brake band slows down the bobbin, and hastens the wind-on of your spun yarn. Experienced spinners require very little tension on the brake band, as they can manipulate their treadling and hand movements to maintain the correct tension.

Release the tension on the brake band when you have finished each day's spinning. This will keep the spring elastic and the nylon cord pliable. The bobbin groove should be very smooth, to allow the free movement of the nylon cord, and light sanding can be helpful if the groove is rough.

Sometimes you may feel that the bobbin is not revolving freely. One reason can be that the maiden uprights are not correctly lined up, and the nylon supports are rubbing on the flyer or bobbin. Correct maintenance and lubrication, as outlined later in this chapter, are also important. If you have made up your own wheel, follow the instructions carefully. I have seen many spinners at the point of giving up, when all that was needed was a small correction in the assembly of the wheel. One would-be spinner, who had not followed the instructions, had glued her brake band tension knob in place, and it would not turn. With a strong twist, I loosened it, and she was transformed into a spinner! Another point to watch is the difference in tension between an empty and a full bobbin. A full bobbin is heavier and greater in circumference than an empty bobbin, and will need more tension.

DOUBLE BELT SYSTEM

This name is somewhat misleading, as the double belt is really a single band which is doubled and crossed in a figure of eight to form both the drive belt and the brake band. The Ashford double belt wheels can be converted to the Scotch tension system, giving the spinner both options on the same wheel.

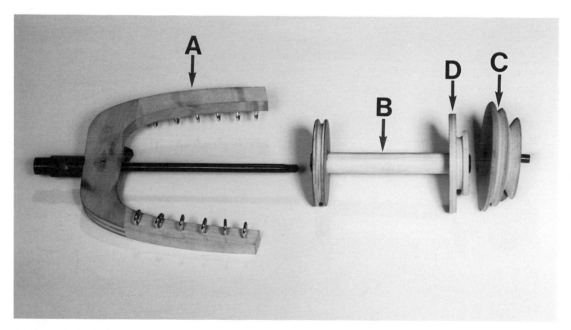

24 Double belt flyer, bobbin and spindle whorl:
A Flyer, B Bobbin, C Spindle whorl, D Bobbin Whorl.

The drive belt section turns the spindle whorl, which is not part of the flyer as it is with the Scotch tension system. It is a separate whorl, which screws onto and turns the shaft, which turns the flyer. The other section of the belt turns the bobbin whorl, which is smaller in diameter than the spindle whorl, making the bobbin revolve faster than the flyer.

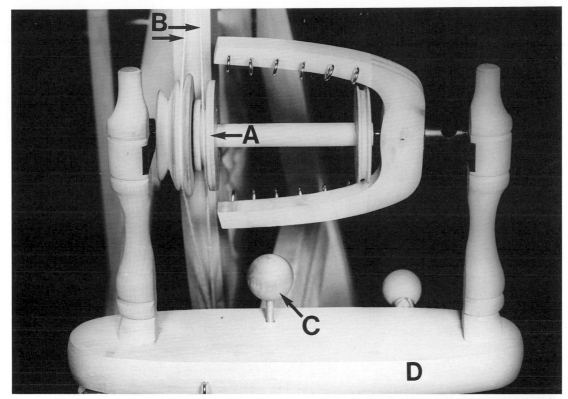

25 Double belt system

A Bobbin whorl C Drive belt tension knob
B Double drive belt D Maiden bar

The groove on the bobbin whorl is U-shaped to allow some slippage, and the groove on the spindle whorl is V-shaped to provide plenty of traction.

As with the Scotch tension system, the spindle whorl has two grooves. The outside groove has a high ratio, for finer spinning than the inside groove.

The tension is altered by turning the drive belt tension knob, which lifts the maiden bar, and tightens the double belt. This causes the spun yarn to wind onto the bobbin at a faster speed, and with less twist. (To tighten the tension on the Elizabeth wheel, read the instructions for this wheel in Appendix B.) When putting the double belt on for the first time, make sure the maiden bar is at its lowest position, and this will allow plenty of take-up when adjusting the tension. Again, a full bobbin requires more tension than an empty bobbin.

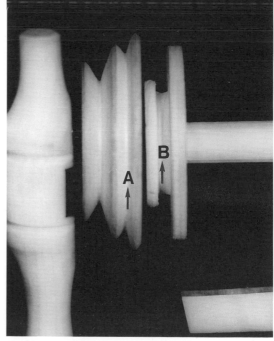

26 V and U-shaped grooves

A Spindle whorl — V-shaped groove
B Bobbin whorl — U-shaped groove

ADVANTAGES AND DISADVANTAGES OF BOTH SYSTEMS

Most beginners find the Scotch tension system easier to understand and control. The separate brake band allows for greater adjustment than the double belt, and lumpy, uneven yarn, and novelty yarn, can be spun onto the bobbin by tightening the Scotch tension. Both bands (the brake and the drive band), can be adjusted separately, to allow for the beginner's hesitancy and lack of co-ordination. The Scotch tension system does lend itself to soft spinning and plying, which also aids the beginner who tends to over-twist the yarn.

The double belt system spins a firmer, more consistent yarn, with more twist, than the Scotch tension system. The double belt needs less of the constant adjusting that is necessary with the other system, as, once the belt is at the correct tension, it needs little attention.

See Appendix B for a description of Ashford wheels and accessories.

MAINTENANCE OF WHEELS

After assembly, staining and polishing, your new spinning wheel should be oiled immediately, before use. A heavy oil that will be retained around the bearings is best.

Con Rod &
Crank Bearing

Flyer Bearings

Fig. 4:2 Oiling the wheel

Apply drops of oil to:
- wheel support bearings;
- connecting rod bearings;
- treadle rail metals;
- flyer bearings, spindle, and any other moving parts.

Do not oil the holes in the wheel hub. Repeat applications of oil after every two to three hours of spinning.

Bobbins

If the bobbin does not run smoothly and quietly, apply a little oil or vaseline to the flyer shaft. If this does not help, the bobbin may be a fraction too tight. A bobbin can be reamed out in the centre with a 6mm (¼in) round file, or tightly-rolled sandpaper.

Drive Belt

If the drive belt slips, yet the tension appears correct, rub beeswax or resin on the belt. Check that the belt is correctly aligned with the spindle whorl. With time and use all drive belts stretch. If the maiden bar is at its highest position, and the drive belt is still too loose, it is time to put on a new belt, or re tie the old one. Return the maiden bar to its lowest position and re-tie or splice the belt, as in Figure 4:1.

Hooks

These will eventually wear, and little grooves will form in the metal to catch the yarn as it passes over the hooks. Replace with new hooks.

Wheel

If the wheel slips on a polished floor, attach rubber feet, or rubber washers to the feet of the spinning wheel. When treadling, push down, not out, and wear flat, non-slip shoes.

Check that the wheel revolves easily. With the drive belt removed, the wheel should continue revolving for some time after you have stopped treadling. If this does not happen, check the wheel and flyer unit for mis-alignment or obstructions.

Orifice

The grease and dirt from the wool will eventually build up inside the orifice, and slow down the passage of the yarn. Clean the inside of the orifice with a cotton bud or soft cloth, dipped in methylated spirits. Do not use any type of scraper or abrasive to clean the orifice, as this will roughen it and cause the yarn to catch.

Careful maintenance of your spinning wheel will repay you many times over. Your wheel will last longer, your spinning will improve, and your enjoyment will increase.

CHAPTER FIVE

Other Spinning Techniques

Worsted yarn · Woollen yarn · Worsted/woollen yarn · Speed spinning · Plying · Fine and bulky spinning · Measuring yarn size · Twists per cm (in) · Determining the twist · Control of twist · Fine spinning · Bulky spinning · Other methods of spinning: short backward draft, short forward draft, medium draft, long draw.

There are two types of yarn that can be handspun: worsted and woollen yarn. These terms have been borrowed from the wool spinning industry and adapted by handspinners. Most handspinners do not have the equipment or knowledge to do true worsted and woollen spinning. However, these two types of yarn, when handspun, still bear enough resemblance to the original processes, for the names to be valid.

WORSTED YARN

This type of yarn is usually spun from long-stapled fleeces. The staples are combed into a parallel formation, which removes all the short fibres. With bought sliver most of this preparation will have been done for you. With fleece wool, unless it is exceptionally clean and free from cotting, it will need combing or flick carding to open the staple, as described in Chapter Three. The staple is spun from the butt end, keeping the fibres parallel at all times. The method of spinning, described in Chapter One, the short backward draft, can be used to spin a worsted yarn. Another method, the short forward draft, is the traditional method for worsted, and is described later in this chapter.

The point to remember when spinning worsted yarn, whichever method is used, is that the fibres should be drafted and then twisted, the two actions being quite separate. A worsted yarn is usually plied, and should be smooth and lustrous. When plying, smooth the yarn between the front thumb and forefinger to flatten any protruding fibres. The yarn is strong and hard-wearing, and is suitable for weaving fabric for men's suiting, or any other smooth, strong cloth. It can also be knitted into hard-wearing garments, such as men's outdoor jerseys.

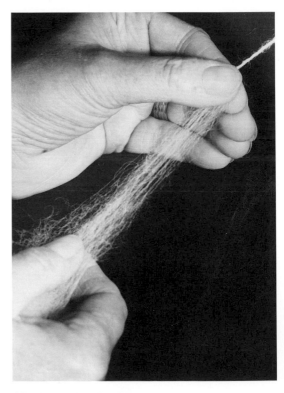

27 Worsted spinning

WOOLLEN YARN

Woollen yarn is usually spun from short-stapled fleeces. The fleece wool should be prepared by carding, and rolling into rolags. Hand carders (Chapter Three, photos **18a-i**), or a drum carder (photos **20a-j**) can be used for this. If wool sliver is used, it can be prepared as in photo **20j**.

Woollen spinning is designed to spin the wool just as the rolag is formed; that is, as a coil of yarn encircling an air pocket. The method used is either the medium draft, or the long draw, both described later in this chapter. With both these methods, the twist is allowed to run into the drafting area, unlike worsted spinning. Try both methods and use the one you find easiest.

Woollen-spun yarn is used for blankets, tweeds and coat fabrics; all cloth that needs fulling, a process that contracts the yarn, and forms a strong warm fabric. Woollen yarn is also used for soft, fluffy, light-weight knitted garments, which will not be subjected to hard wear.

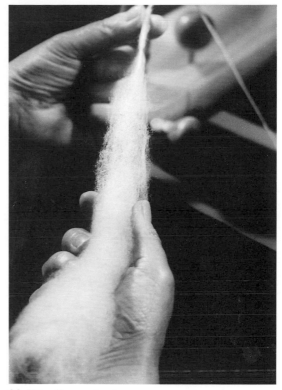

28 Woollen spinning

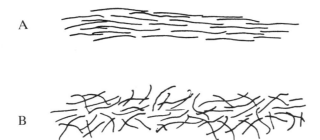

Fig. 5:1 Worsted and woollen yarn.

WORSTED/WOOLLEN YARN

Handspinners have developed a mixture of worsted/woollen yarn, which is halfway between the two processes. I have used this type of yarn for a soft, light-weight indoor jersey for myself, because it stands up to hard wear better than woollen spinning, yet is softer in touch than worsted spinning. The fleece or sliver is prepared by folding the staple or sliver over your forefinger and spinning from the fold.

Use either the short backward/forward draft, or for a softer yarn, the medium draft method of spinning.

These three types, worsted, woollen, and worsted/woollen yarn, may seem confusing at first, but it is valuable to experiment with them, when you have mastered the basic spinning techniques. The ability to spin worsted and woollen yarns will widen the scope of your spinning, and enable you to make a much greater range of garments with the spun yarn. You will also learn how to control the wheel and your hand movements to become the master of the wheel, not its slave. It is surprising how many spinners use one method of spinning and one type of fleece all their lives, and the longer they do this, the harder it is to change. I know of spinners who use only Romney wool and the worsted method of spinning using the short forward draw. Of course, they are experts in that field, but what a lot they are missing!

29 Spinning from the fold

SPEED SPINNING

As you become more proficient your spinning will naturally become faster. However, here are some hints that will help those who wish to spin quickly.

A. Use good quality, clean, greasy wool. Greasy sliver will also hasten the process, as it needs no preparation. Spinning in the sun, or by a warm fire softens the grease in the wool, and makes it easier to spin.

B. Check that your wheel is in good condition, well oiled and running smoothly. It should be stable on the floor, and not rock when you are treadling quickly.

C. A large drive wheel lets you spin quickly without treadling frantically. Check that the drive ratio is suitable for the thickness of the yarn you wish to spin. It is tiring to fight against the natural setting of your wheel.

D. The bobbin should hold a reasonable amount of yarn, and be quick and easy to change.

E. Learn to join the yarn, and to pick out seeds or dirt without stopping the wheel. The slippage on the brake band allows you to hold back the yarn fractionally while you do this.

F. Learn to stop the wheel with the crankshaft in a 1 o'clock position for spinning and an 11 o'clock position for plying. This allows you to begin treadling without taking your hands off the wool.

G. Some spinning techniques are quicker than others. Both the medium draft and the long draw are quick spinning methods, as they have fewer hand movements than other methods. A one-handed method, described in Paula Simmon's book *Spinning for Softness and Speed* (Madrona Publishers, Seattle, U.S.A), is excellent for speed spinning.

Do not sacrifice quality for quantity in this process of speed spinning. It is not worth it!

PLYING

Experienced spinners can use another method of plying to produce a well-rounded yarn. Ply with the hands in the normal position, as described in Chapter One, but allow the singles to relax as they are plied. The two strands will hang loosely between the two hands instead of being taut. Ply with a very light tension, and take great care that one strand of singles does not wrap itself around the other. As there is no pressure on the relaxed singles while plying they tend to kink and twist and may be difficult to manage. Leave the singles on the bobbins overnight before plying. This sets the yarn, and makes it easier to control.

FINE AND BULKY SPINNING

It is not long before any beginner wants to change the thickness of the yarn. For the first few weeks (or even months) just spinning an even yarn is the main aim, but once this goal is achieved you will want to try spinning a thicker or thinner yarn.

There are three components when changing the yarn diameter.

Fleece
Each fleece seems to have a yarn diameter that comes naturally to it. This depends on the crimp pattern and fibre diameter. A fine, soft Merino fleece will naturally spin a fine, soft yarn. A coarse fleece, such as a Lincoln, will naturally spin a thicker yarn. Learn to judge this quality in a fleece, and spin accordingly.

Wheel
A wheel such as the Elizabeth, with drive ratios of 8.5:1 and 12.5:1 will spin a finer yarn, with more twist, than a Traditional wheel. The bulky spinner, with a ratio of 2.9:1 will spin a thick yarn with less twist. Choose the right wheel for the yarn size.

Spinning technique
The tension, speed of drafting and treadling, and the amount of wool in the draft, will determine the size of the yarn.

MEASURING YARN SIZE

This has been a difficult question for spinners. Yarn has traditionally been divided into three classes, fine, medium and bulky. But how thick is a bulky yarn? What is termed a medium yarn? In the past, a weight per length system has been used, with varying success. With this system 100gm of fine yarn would measure 400-800m. However, this system is being replaced by the 'wraps per cm' (wraps per in) method. This indicates how many times the spun yarn can be wound around a ruler for 2.5cm (1in). The yarn is wound with each thread touching the next, but not crammed. Do not stretch the wool in the winding process.

Do not count the first few wraps, as they will not be accurate, but then count the number of wraps for 2.5cm (1in).

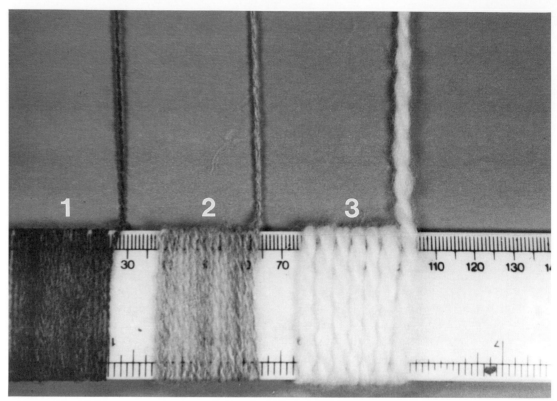

30 Wraps per cm (1in)
1 Fine yarn, 24 wraps per 2.5cm (1in)
2 Medium yarn, 14 wraps per 2.5cm (1in)
3 Bulky yarn, 7 wraps per 2.5cm (1in)

TABLE 1: YARNS

Type of wool (Plied)	Wraps per 2.5cm (1in)	Equivalent in commercial wool	Appropriate drive ratio	Twists per 2.5cm (1in)	Twist angle
Fine	More than 20	2 and 3 ply	9-13:1	10-17	25°-45°
Medium	12-20	4 ply and double knit	5-10:1	5-10	15°-25°
Bulky	Less than 12	bulky and triple knit	3-6:1	1-4	5°-15°

These figures are guidelines only. An 'Anne Field Law', which I have just invented, indicates that wraps per 2.5cm (1in) are approximately double the number of twists per 2.5cm (1in).

The advantage of the 'wraps per cm (in)' method is that you can check the yarn size as soon as you begin spinning. With the old system, you had to wait until you had wound the yarn onto a niddy noddy and weighed it. The knitting patterns at the end of the book will size the yarn by the wrapping method.

TWISTS PER CM (IN)

Experienced spinners can spin an even yarn of a suitable thickness and with the same number of twists per cm (in) for a complete project. When asked how they do this, they will tell you by 'feel' or by instinct. Less experienced spinners, in building up this 'feel', will need some help. Unfortunately, there are no hard and fast rules, but there are some guidelines. A fine fleece, should be spun into a fine yarn, with more twists per cm (in) than a coarser fleece. If a fine fleece is spun fine but loosely, it will break. If a coarse fleece is spun tightly, it will be stringy and harsh to handle. The ability to assess fleece characteristics of fineness and crimp pattern is a great help when deciding the diameter and twists per cm (in) of your yarn. Another factor to take into account is the wearing qualities needed in the finished article. A high-twist yarn is harder wearing than a soft-twist yarn.

DETERMINING THE TWIST PER CM (IN)

There are three methods.

Doubling
While spinning the singles, pull some of the spun yarn off the bobbin and allow it to twist back on itself, as in photo **7**, Chapter One. This doubled portion will indicate the twist count and thickness of the plied yarn. It also allows for the slight untwisting that takes place when plying. Adjust your spinning, making the yarn thicker/thinner or more/less twisted, until the desired yarn is achieved. Then knot and break off the doubled length of this yarn as a sample and use this as a reference throughout the entire project. This sample can be sized, using the wraps per cm (in) method, and the twists per cm (in) counted, if absolute accuracy is necessary.

Crimp pattern
Count the crimps per cm (in) in a staple of your fleece wool. Then spin with the same number of twists per cm (in). The crimp pattern is the natural wave or twist in the wool fibre. By matching this with your spun yarn, you are following the inherent characteristics of that fibre. In sliver wool, the crimp pattern has been modified, making it difficult to count, and other methods of determining the twist should be used.

Angle of twist
A more scientific method of measuring the twist is now being used by many spinners. The diagonal angle the twist makes in relation to the length of the yarn can be measured. The tighter the twist, the greater the angle.

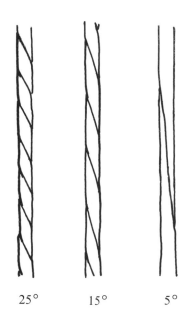

25°   15°   5°

Fig. 5:2 Angle of twist

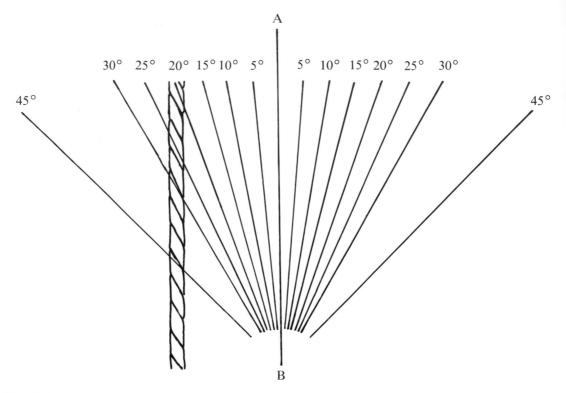

Fig. 5:3 Measuring the twist angle

Take a length of spun yarn, holding it firmly to prevent the twist unwinding. Lay the yarn parallel to the centre line in Figure **5:3**. A magnifying glass may be needed for very fine wool. Determine the angle of twist in your yarn. The yarn illustrated has a twist angle of 25°. For each bobbin, until that particular project is finished, spin with the same twist angle.

5° = very soft twist
10° = soft twist
15° = soft/medium twist
20° = medium twist
25° = hard/medium twist
30° = hard twist
45° = very hard twist

CONTROL OF TWIST

Once you have determined the desired thickness and twist per cm (in) (**t.p.cm.(in)**), it is now necessary to put the same number of t.p.cm(in) in the yarn for the entire project. Only with very small projects can enough wool be spun in one sitting. Yet each time you sit at the wheel your mood will be different, and even the weather affects your spinning. A cold day may prevent the grease from flowing in the wool and your hands may not be as dexterous.

To control the twist
A. Count the number of treadle pushes to one draft.
B. Measure the length of the draft; i.e. the distance between your hands.
C. Gauge the amount of wool in each draft. For example, I could be spinning with one draft to four pushes of the treadle, with 10cm (4in) in each draft. The amount I gauge by eye. Next time I sit at the wheel I use the same timing.

Of course there will be variations, as we are not machines, but once this rhythm is established, a consistent yarn can be spun.

Plying

Most spinners ply with the same amount of t.p.cm(in) as they put into the singles. This gives the yarn a balanced twist, as described in Chapter One. Use the same method of control: counting and measuring the length of your draft, as you did when spinning the singles.

Drive ratio

Use the correct wheel for the thickness and twist of the yarn. For example, if you normally spin a medium yarn, with fourteen wraps and seven twists per 2.5cm (1in), a wheel with a drive ratio of 6.6:1 would be suitable. On this wheel, for one treadle, 6.6 twists are put into the yarn. Therefore, if you feed 2.5cm (1in) of yarn onto the bobbin for one treadle, the correct number of twists will be inserted. Of course, if you spin 5cm (2in) of yarn for two treadles, the result will be the same.

However, if you usually spin bulky yarns, with eight wraps and three twists per 2.5cm (1in), a wheel with a drive ratio of 3.4:1 would be more suitable. For one treadle, that is, one revolution of the drive wheel, three to four twists are put into the amount of yarn fed onto the bobbin. If your wheel has a ratio of 10:1, it is very difficult to put only three twists into 2.5cm (1in). To do so means feeding 8cm (3in) of yarn in each draft for one treadle — an almost impossible task!

To find the number of cm (in) that should be fed into the bobbin for each treadle, divide the drive ratio of the wheel by the twists per cm (in). Table 1 gives some guidelines for appropriate drive ratios. If you find all this discussion about drive ratios confusing, re-read the information in Chapter 4.

FINE SPINNING

Fine spinning can be defined as having more than twenty wraps per 2.5cm (1in).

Fleece

Choose a fleece at the fine end of the breed range. For your first attempt a Merino fleece may be too difficult — a Polwarth or a Corriedale fleece would be wiser. If buying sliver, choose a quarterbred or halfbred class. Pull a few fibres out from the wool, study the crimp pattern, and twist these fibres a few times. Make some decisions on the size of the yarn from these observations. Decide on which spinning type to use.

The following description is for spinning a worsted yarn, using either the short forward or backward draft. A woollen yarn, using either the medium or long draw spinning method, is the traditional method for short-stapled, fine wools. Although this is a worsted method of spinning, the breed wool and the spinning technique enable a soft, airy yarn to be spun.

Wheel

Put the drive belt onto the smallest whorl because a high ratio, from 8-15:1, is necessary for fine spinning. On page 131 are instructions for obtaining a ratio of 15:1. Adjust the drive belt tension on this new whorl. Fine yarn needs more twist and lighter tension than bulky wool.

Loosen the tension on the Scotch brake/ double drive belt. Very fine wool is best spun with a very fine drive belt, and this may need changing. If this fine belt slips, rub resin onto it. Another way to keep the tension very light is to use a partly-filled bobbin, and spin only from the back flyer hooks.

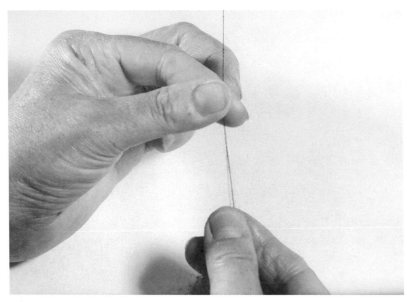

31 Fine spinning

Spinning technique

Although spinning fine yarn is a slow process, a little yarn goes a long way so do not despair. There are three points to remember:

A. Slow down your hand movements to allow more twist to gather in the yarn. If the yarn keeps breaking, there is not enough twist; if it kinks and curls into a hard knot, there is too much twist. As it is a weightless yarn, expect more kinking than you would find in a normal yarn. It will help to count as you spin, to ensure that the same number of twists are inserted in each drafting move. (Try '1 and 2 and 3 and 4 and 5 and **go**.' At 'go', let the yarn move onto the bobbin).

B. Quicken your treadling speed.

C. The type of fleece or sliver used for fine spinning will be a fine, tightly-crimped fleece. Spinning this closely-crimped wool with a light tension will not straighten the crimp. In normal spinning the tension pulls the crimp out of the yarn as you spin. However, with fine spinning and little tension the crimp may become trapped in the twisted yarn causing it to lose elasticity and to shrink and felt. Prevent this by holding the fibres straight and uncrimped between the front and back hands as the drafted fibres are twisted. The best way to do this is to lower the back hand below the front hand, which angles the wool downwards. This puts tension on the fibres in the drafting area, and straightens them.

Test the yarn, by pulling some spun yarn off the bobbin, and let it double over. This will be the size of the plied yarn. This doubled strand should be translucent and airy. You will feel that you are putting too much twist into the yarn, but remember, when plying, there will be as much twist put in the opposite direction, undoing some of the original twist.

Plying

The high twist in fine wool can make it less manageable when plying. If the yarn is left to set on the bobbin overnight it will be easier to ply, and there will be no little curls, like pigs' tails, poking out of the plied yarn. Give the plied yarn an equal amount of twist as the singles, by using the same count per draft. Ply with the wool angled downwards, as in spinning, to tension the singles and straighten the crimp. Wind into small skeins, using half of the niddy noddy, to prevent tangling while washing.

BULKY SPINNING

Bulky wool has fewer than twelve wraps per 2.5cm (1in).

Fleece

Choose a strong fleece, such as a Lincoln or English Leicester. If using sliver choose a strong crossbred type. Pull a few fibres out, and study the crimp pattern and fibre size. There will be little crimp in this range of wool, which means the spun yarn will have little elasticity. Twist a few strands and decide on the approximate size of yarn you feel will suit that particular fleece. Decide which spinning method to use, thinking of the finished article. Worsted spinning is traditionally used for these long-stapled wools, using either the short forward/backward draft. Prepare the wool accordingly.

Wheel

Put the drive belt on the largest spindle whorl for a low drive ratio of 2-5:1. A jumbo flyer may be the best way to achieve this ratio. Bulky yarn needs less twist than fine yarn, so increase the Scotch brake (or double belt) tension. A thick drive belt may also help this tighter tension. Check that the orifice is large enough to accommodate the thicker yarn.

Spinning technique

This is the opposite of fine spinning.
A. Quicken your hand movements, allowing less twist into the yarn.
B. Slow your treadling speed.

The counting system, as described in fine spinning, can regulate the amount of twist. Test the yarn by pulling some of it off the bobbin,

32 Bulky spinning

and doubling it over. Again it should be light and airy. If it is a dense, heavy yarn, a jersey knitted with it will be too heavy. I once had a student who spun and knitted her husband a jersey which weighed over 1.4kg (3lbs)!

Plying

Count when plying, to match the count used while spinning the bulky singles. This will ensure equal twist in the spun and plied yarn. Wash normally.

OTHER METHODS OF SPINNING

I mentioned earlier in this chapter that there are ways of spinning other than the method used in Chapter One, the short backward draft. This is probably the most common method among spinners, and, as it leads easily to other techniques, it seems the best for beginners. However, there are other methods that can be used. All these spinning methods seem very separate and arbitrary, when laid down in a list. If you go to a spinning day attended by twenty spinners, you will find twenty different methods of spinning, with each of those twenty all knowing they have the right way. Each spinner has adapted the basic spinning methods to suit his/her dexterity, his/her wheel, type of wool, and the finished article. Practise all the methods and then you will have a similar range of choice, and can make an informed decision on your own spinning method, for each separate project.

SHORT BACKWARD DRAFT

I will briefly summarize this method, described in Chapter One, photos **6a-f**. The front hand, usually the left hand, remains stationary, with the thumb and forefinger opening to let the twist through to the drafted fibres, then pinching to allow the back hand to draft. The back hand, usually the right, holds the loose fibres, drafts them into a fan shape and then brings the drafted, and now twisted fibres up to let them run onto the bobbin. This method is suitable for worsted spinning.

SHORT FORWARD DRAFT

This is another common method of spinning. Many beginners use this method and change to the short backward draft when they have more experience. However, it does not lead easily to other methods of spinning, and if used for a long time, a spinner may have difficulty in changing. The process is the reverse of the short backward draft. The front hand does all the work.

This is the traditional way to spin worsted wool, as the twisted and the drafted sections never overlap.

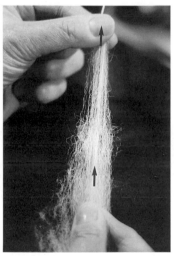

33a The front hand drafts from the loose fibres, held in the back hand, pinching with thumb and fore-finger to keep the twist out of the drafted area.

33b Release the pinch, to allow the twist to run into the drafted area.

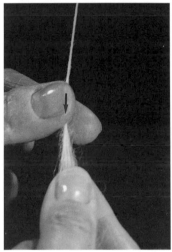

33c The front hand moves back, smoothing the yarn as it does so, and keeping pace with the twist.

MEDIUM DRAFT

This is an extension of the short backward draft.

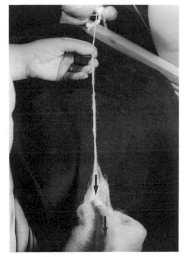

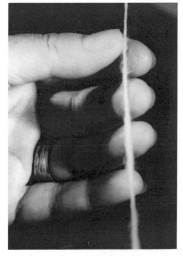

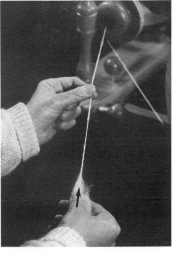

34a The back hand drafts back as the twist is let into the drafting area, keeping pace with the twist and a little ahead.

34b The front hand does not pinch, as this would not let the twist into the drafted area. It supports the yarn, occasionally gripping it to allow the drafting hand something to pull against when thicker or more stubborn places occur.

34c When the yarn is the correct thickness and twist, bring the back hand forward to let the yarn run onto the bobbin.

This is a quick spinning method, but one which requires good fleece preparation, as the wool must flow freely from the back hand. Good sliver wool can be spun easily using this method. Fleece wool should be well carded or combed. This method is used for woollen spinning, as the drafted and twisted sections overlap, and there is no pinching by the front hand to expel the air from the spun yarn.

When I am really showing off, to impress my students, I spin this way, using only one hand.

35 Me, showing off

This sounds like something done in the wild west, but it is really a spinning method, used for woollen spinning. The back hand changes direction for the first time and works across the body, at a right-angle to the front hand.

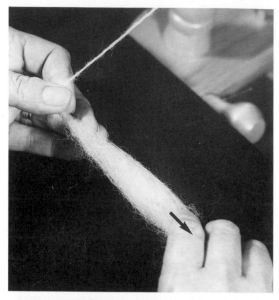

36a The front hand, usually the left, stays about 10cm (4in) from the orifice. It pinches the yarn, to let the twist accumulate in front of this hand.

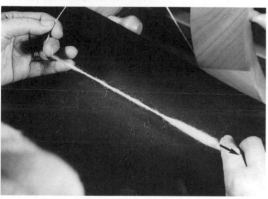

36b The back hand drafts the fibres across the body width. Some twist is let through into the drafting fibres to give them strength. About 5cm (2in) of loose fibre will be in front of the back hand. Do not allow more fibre into the drafting area as you draft back.

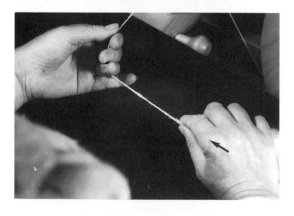

36c When the yarn is the desired thickness and twist, the pinch is released by the front hand, and the yarn brought forward to wind onto the bobbin. Again, as with the medium draft, the wool must be well prepared.

CHAPTER SIX

Novelty Yarns and Other Fibres

Novelty yarns: flecks, slubs, bead and knot yarn, Navaho plying, crepe, squeezed yarn •
Spinning with other fibres: cotton, silk, flax, mohair, angora rabbit hair, hemp, jute, ramie,
sisal, dog hair, alpaca, camel hair, cashmere.

Novelty yarns, with their textured character, are fun to spin as they are so unlike the even yarn you have been endeavouring to produce so far. In spinning these novelty yarns you will consolidate much of the knowledge you have already gained, and learn to do some new 'tricks' on the wheel. This should make you more comfortable with the wheel and appreci-ative of its range. The novelty yarns themselves are useful for weaving, knitting and crochet. You will probably only spin small amounts using the slower techniques, but even small amounts of textured yarn can add much interest to a garment. Quicker techniques, such as 'flecks' can be used for a whole garment.

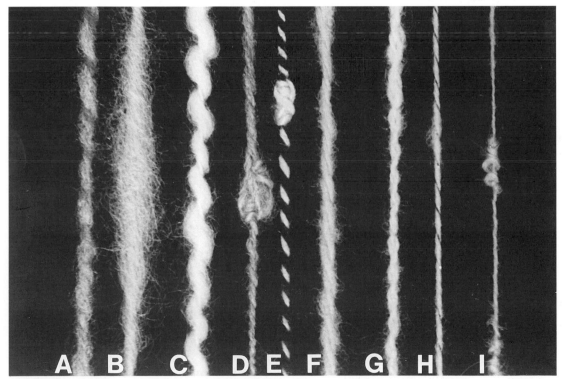

37 Novelty yarns:
A Flecks, B Slub (singles), C Bead yarn, D Knot yarn, E Knot yarn (silk and wool), F Navaho plying,
G Crepe yarn, H Lurex and wool, I Squeezed yarn.

FLECKS

These are short pieces of wool inserted while plying. These insertions can be coloured tops, scoured sliver, staples from contrasting fleece wool, or pieces of camel hair, silk top, etc. First spin two bobbins of singles. When plying, add the flecks at the V where the twisting takes place. Ply with one hand, and add the flecks with the other, either randomly or at regular intervals. Flecks can also be added at right-angles to the plied yarn to form tufts. Wash normally.

38 Flecks

SLUBS

Slub yarn can be spun as a singles or as a plied yarn, and the slubs can be regular or random. It may seem odd to be trying to put slubs back into the yarn, when for months you have been trying to get rid of them! To insert the slubs, pinch the yarn between the front forefinger and thumb in the drafted area, not at the meeting place of the drafted and twisted yarn as formerly. This will put a lump or slub of unspun yarn into your thread.

When plying two slub yarns together two slubs may end up on top of each other and this very thick part may not pull through the orifice. It is better to ply the slub singles with a normal handspun singles. I have seen a very effective yarn made of a slub singles plied with a commercial cotton thread, and there are other variations.

39 Inserting slubs

BEAD YARN

This is where your knowledge of S and Z spun yarns, as explained on page 21, will come in handy. Spin a fine singles yarn with an S twist. On another bobbin spin a bulky yarn with a Z twist. Ply the two together with an S twist, retarding the fine yarn, and letting the bulky yarn wrap itself around the fine. Plying S gives more twist to the fine yarn, and less twist to the bulky, thus accentuating the size difference even further.

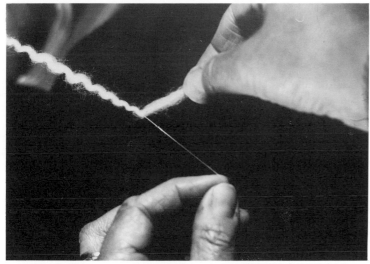

40 Bead yarn

KNOT YARN

Spin two singles with a Z twist. When plying S, hold the singles in separate hands, and wind one singles around the other in a figure of eight. Make the knots with alternate singles, to ensure that equal amounts will be plied from each bobbin.

CREPE YARN

Spin four singles Z twist, using a worsted spin for a smooth, lustrous yarn. First ply one pair of the singles together, then the other pair, both in an S direction with a high twist. You will now have two bobbins of two ply yarn. Ply these two together with a moderate Z twist.

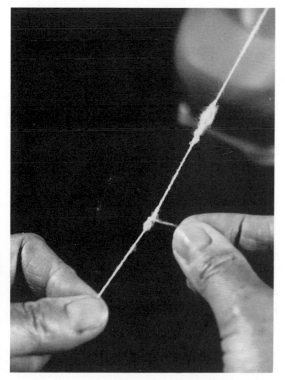

41 Knot yarn

This is a useful way to make a 3-ply yarn from a singles, using only one bobbin. The singles yarn is chained in loops to form the triple yarn. Spin a singles Z twist.

Fasten the beginning of the singles to the leader and ply with an S twist, chaining as you do so. Chain with the back hand, letting the front hand pinch and release the twist in the usual manner. The loops of the chain do not have to be the same length, but they should be at least 20cm (8in) long for ease of handling. When you have mastered the chaining technique, try spinning the singles in different colours, and then ply and chain with the loops matching the colour changes. This is an excellent way to spin a multi-coloured yarn.

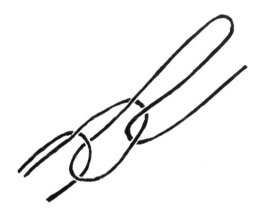

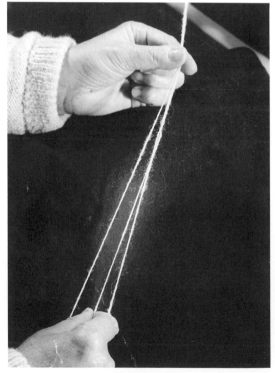

Fig. 6:1 Navaho plying

42a 42b Navaho plying

SQUEEZED YARN

Spin two singles Z twist. When plying S, every now and then push one singles up the other thread to form a bunch. This is most effective with two contrasting colours.

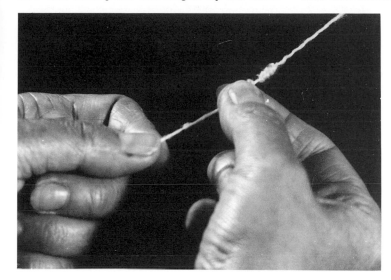

43 Squeezed yarn

ADDITION OF COMMERCIAL YARN WHILE PLYING

Many variations, using commercial yarn, are possible. Lurex and wool is one good combination for stoles, shawls and women's jerseys for evening wear.

A light, fluffy handspun yarn, plied with a fine commercial sewing cotton, with the cotton retarded as in bead yarn, is effective. The range is limited only by your imagination.

SPINNING OTHER FIBRES

It is commonly believed that spinning wheels are for spinning wool only, yet flax spinning has been popular for centuries. Many other fibres can be spun into yarn, and it is fun to try different types. Almost any hair or fibre can be spun into some type of yarn and in experimenting with other fibres, your spinning technique will certainly improve.

Today we can buy most of these fibres already prepared for spinning, and this does save much time as the preparation can be a long and tedious process. In most cases the fibre will have been cleaned, washed and carded into a type of sliver. This makes it good value for the spinner as there is little wastage. Manufacturers sell these prepared fibres as slivers, tops or rovings. Amongst spinners these names have become almost interchangeable, although there are differences (see Glossary).

Not only can these fibres be used on their own, but they can be blended or plied with wool to produce interesting yarns. (See 'Blending' in Chapter Three.) For example, silk and wool plied together give a yarn with added lustre as the silk catches the light.

COTTON

Cotton is available in a sliver, ready to spin, and this is the most manageable form for the beginner as the cotton fibres are very short in length. Put the drive belt onto the smaller spindle whorl to increase the drive ratio — cotton needs more twist than wool — and spin with a light tension. Short, swift drafting movements are necessary if you are spinning with the short forward or backward draft. The long draw method is also used by many cotton spinners.

The finished yarn will probably look over-twisted even when care is taken. This disappears with washing, and weighting the cotton yarn while drying will also remove this extra twist. To weight the skein, put a piece of wood through the loop at the lower end of two skeins, or if you are drying only one skein, tie a weight to the lower loop. Move the weight around the skein at intervals.

Handspun cotton yarn is usually more uneven than wool yarn, but the texture adds to the interest. Cotton dyes readily with plant and chemical dyes. Cotton yarn can be used in knitting, crochet, and weaving, particularly in hot climates, where wool is not suitable.

44 Cotton sliver (right) and spun cotton (plied cotton, left and singles)

45 Spinning with cotton

SILK

Silk, with its long, almost continuous fibre, is so easy to spin that it seems to spin itself. Bought sliver varies in colour from white to beige. Tussah, or wild silk, comes from wild, not cultivated silkworms, and is the darker shade. The loose form of silk breaks easily but it is very strong when spun. The yarn has little elasticity, and is smooth and lustrous. It can be used as a singles, plied, or plied with other fibres such as wool or cotton.

Wash the skeins gently in warm, soapy water, avoiding squeezing and overhandling. Rinse carefully, with a little vinegar added to the rinsing water. The vinegar helps to preserve the sheen, which can be dulled with washing, and also gives silk that characteristic squeaky sound. Another method of preserving the sheen, and also preventing the yarn from further stretching, is done after the final rinse. Insert a thin rod in one end of the skein, and turn the rod around and around until the skein is tightly twisted. Remove the rod, put your hands in both ends of the skein and snap it apart a few times, moving your hands around the skein as you do so. This snapping can also be done during the drying time.

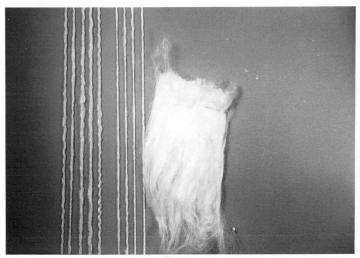

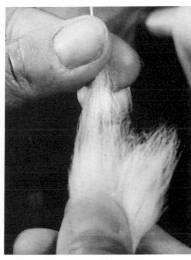

46 Silk sliver (right) and spun silk (plied Tussah silk, left and Ching Chiang silk)

47 Spinning with silk

FLAX

This fibre comes from the flax plant, of which there are many varieties. *Linum usitatissimum* is a fine variety — choose an appropriate type for the finished article.

Flax comes in two forms, line or tow. Line flax is strong and shiny, with very long fibres. Tow is in short lengths, is not as smooth, and can be broken readily. This fibre needs long and arduous processing to make it suitable for spinning. Buying prepared flax will save much time and there is a wide choice from coarse to fine, bleached to water-retted, and white to beige. Linen is the yarn or cloth woven from flax, and sometimes these terms are confused, with the prepared fibre being called linen flax, or linen top.

Traditionally flax is spun from a distaff, a long peg sited above the flyer unit, from which the fibre is drawn and then spun. Line flax is more suitable for distaff spinning than tow. An Ashford distaff can be purchased which screws onto the three Traditional wheels.

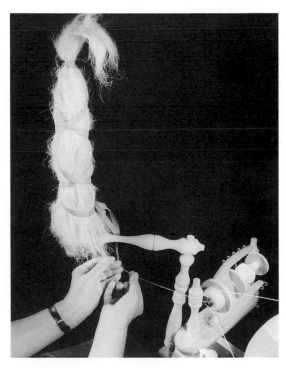

48 Spinning flax from an Ashford distaff

NOVELTY YARNS AND OTHER FIBRES 65

49 Prepared flax (right) and spun flax (plied flax, left, and flax and silk plied together).

To prepare the flax for distaff spinning, first break off a length of flax sliver about 46cm (18in) long. This is called a 'strick'.

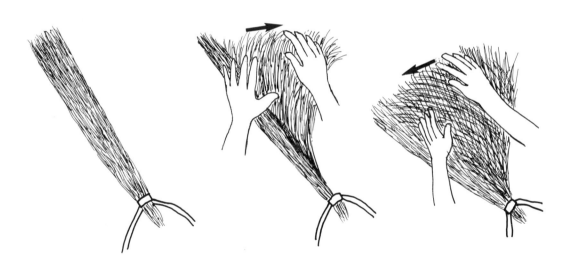

Fig. 6:2 Sit at a table, and lay the strick near your left hand. Tie the end of the strick nearest to you securely, and then take the ends of the cords around your waist and tie them.

Take some fibres from the strick, move them to the right, and begin fanning them out in a right to left movement. Continue this fanning out, crossing back and forth. Let the fibres cross each other, rather than lie parallel, as this will make for easier spinning. When all the fibres are fanned out, untie the cord from your waist and undo the tie around the flax. Place the distaff along at the end nearest to you. Wind the fan around the distaff from left to right. Sometimes tissue paper is first wound around the distaff as padding.

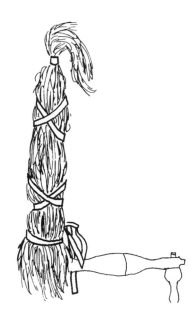

Secure the flax with a ribbon, beginning at the top of the distaff and finishing at the lower end, crossing on the way. When you are spinning, the fibres should run smoothly from the distaff.

It is not necessary to use a distaff when spinning flax, although the fibres seem to run with greater ease if you do. The fibre can be held on the lap as with wool spinning. However, there are essential differences in spinning with flax. Flax should be moistened as it is spun, so have a bowl of water handy and wet the fingers of your front hand regularly while spinning. This will strengthen and smooth the hairy texture of the yarn. Flax is harsh and cool to handle, in comparison with the warmth and elasticity of wool. It has no elasticity but it is extremely hard wearing, softening and becoming more flexible with age. Flax is such a strong fibre it should be spun with little twist and with a light tension.

Finished garments or articles should be ironed while wet to produce the crisp, shiny finish associated with linen. However, linen cloth should not be ironed over the folds, as sharp creasing will break the fibres.

The crisp handle of flax yarn makes it more suitable for weaving than for knitting or crochet. However, a plied yarn of flax and wool can be used for a wide range of garments, as it is softer and more elastic.

MOHAIR

Mohair, the fibre from the Angora goat, is soft, lustrous and non-elastic. A light card with a flick carder is usually all that is needed to prepare it for spinning. Mohair should be spun as for wool, using the worsted method for a strong, smooth yarn, and the woollen method for a soft, fluffy yarn. Spin with slightly more twist than wool, and with a light tension. Mohair is often blended with wool on drum or handcarders before spinning, as the mohair component adds a soft, luxurious feel to the wool. A blend of up to 50 per cent mohair, 50 per cent wool, makes easy spinning for the beginner. Use a wool with a matching crimp if blending, as this will be compatible with the mohair.

Leave the yarn on the bobbins for a day or two before plying to make it easier to handle. Weight the skein while drying for the same reason, as explained under the 'Cotton' heading earlier in this chapter. Mohair is also easier to handle if kept in the refrigerator or freezer prior to spinning, as this seems to 'tame' the fibres.

Mohair can also be spun onto a fine hand-spun wool singles, taking care with the twist direction. If the singles is Z spun, then the mohair should be spun onto it with an S twist.

Mohair takes both commercial and plant dyes with a greater depth of colour than wool.

Mohair can be used for knitting, crocheting, and weaving, but care should be taken with the tension. Mohair is heavier than wool, and light, lacy patterns are preferable. Elasticity can be given to the finished garment by knitting a very fine, invisible, elastic thread with the mohair.

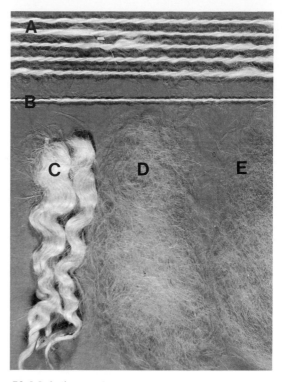

50 Mohair staple and spun mohair
A Mohair
B Fine mohair
C Mohair staples
D Carded mohair
E Carded mohair and wool blend

ANGORA RABBIT HAIR

This fibre is often confused with the hair of the Angora goat (which is called mohair, not angora). Angora hair is soft, short and slippery. The drafting should be short and quick, using the worsted method, with either the short forward or backward draft. Angora can be spun onto a fine commercial wool singles (size 132). This base yarn will not be seen in the finished yarn, but adds strength. Angora hair can also be blended with fine wools, on drum or handcarders, and this will reduce shedding. Angora which has been plucked from the rabbit will shed very little however. Angora yarn is eight times warmer than wool and is best knitted on large needles with an open pattern.

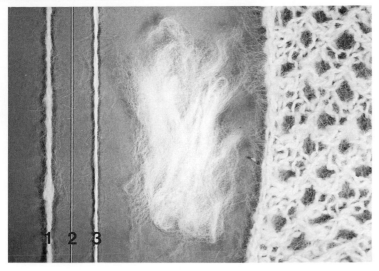

51 Angora rabbit hair, spun yarn, and knitted sample
1 Polwarth and Angora carded together then plied.
2 Commercial wool single, size 132.
3 Angora spun onto the commercial single then plied.

OTHER FIBRES

There are many other fibres that can be spun into yarn. If you are trying a fibre for the first time and are not sure how to go about it, examine the length and the strength of the fibre.

If it is short and breaks easily, spin with plenty of twist, and short, quick drafting movements. If the fibre is long and strong, use less twist, and longer drafting movements.

Hemp
Spin as for flax.

Jute
This is a coarse fibre that rots and yellows with age, and it is not as strong as flax. Do not dampen with water while spinning, but use olive oil to moisten the fibres.

Ramie
This is a very strong, non-elastic vegetable fibre that spins into a soft lustrous yarn. It can be blended with other fibres. Spin as for flax.

Sisal
A coarse vegetable fibre which should be dampened before spinning by rolling in a wet towel for several hours.

Dog combings
Long-haired dogs such as Samoyeds have hair that can be spun into yarn. The hair can be blended with wool before spinning, or plied with wool or other fibres. Oil added before spinning makes the hair more manageable.

Alpaca
The colour ranges from beige to almost black. Spin as for mohair. Alpaca can be blended with wool, on the carders, using up to 50 per cent of wool. It is a strong, non-elastic, lustrous animal fibre.

Camel Hair
This is of two grades. The coarse outer hair spins into a strong, hairy yarn, and the soft downy undercoat spins into a light and fluffy yarn. Moistening the fingers with olive oil will aid spinning. Camel hair can be blended with compatible wools before spinning.

Cashmere
Cashmere comes from the fleece of the Cashmere goat. The soft, downy undercoat of this animal is a luxurious, costly fibre, available in very limited quantities.

CHAPTER SEVEN

Questions and Answers

My yarn is overspun, with little curls, and it feels harsh. How do I remedy this?

Many spinners feel their handspun singles are overspun, particularly if it is a fine yarn. Remember that plying in the opposite direction will undo some of this twist. The washing process, which bulks and fluffs up the yarn, will also reduce some overtwisting. To test your singles yarn for overspinning, pull some off the bobbin, and let it twist back on itself. If the yarn is hard and solid, and has small kinks and curls, it is overspun. Another test is to hold the yarn up to the light. It should be translucent and airy. There is nothing that can be done to this yarn, but next time you are spinning, try the following hints.
1. Gently increase the tension on the brake band (for a Scotch tension wheel) or the drive belt (on a double belt wheel).
2. Quicken your hand movements. It is common for beginners to spin with hand movements too slow for their treadling speed.
3. Slow down your treadling speed. Overspinning happens when your hands and feet do not work at the correct pace in relation to each other. In other words, your treadling is faster than your hands can keep up with.

My wheel is hard to push, and I have to force down on the treadle to get the wheel to move. What is wrong?

Check that the flyer is lined up in a straight line, with the drive belt travelling in a straight line from the wheel to the spindle whorl. Sometimes the nylon bearings can be out of alignment and they scrape on the spindle whorl or the bobbin. Check that the maiden uprights are straight, and not twisted inwards, and that the drive band is not too tight.

The wheel may need oiling. See Figure 4:2, Chapter Four for oiling directions.

My drive belt keeps jumping off the wheel. How do I prevent this?

Make sure the flyer is lined up, with the drive belt travelling in a straight line from the wheel to the spindle whorl. A large knot or a loose end in the drive belt will also throw the belt off the wheel. When starting the wheel by hand, use the spokes for the initial push, not the rim of the wheel.

I want to spin a warp yarn for weaving. Is there anything special I should be doing?

As the warp yarn is under tension on the loom, it needs to be strong. However, wool is such an adaptable fibre that it is not as difficult as you would think. Spin with slightly more twist than usual, and spin a smooth yarn, with no slubs or lumps to catch in the heddles or reed. Take care with joining in both spinning and plying, as weak places will pull apart on the loom. Spread the join over 8-10cm (3-4in) to make it strong. Test for strength by pulling a piece of the yarn over your thumbnail. It should not break until some pressure is applied. A plied yarn will be stronger than a singles yarn. When choosing a fleece, consider the end use of the article, as you would when knitting. A soft knee rug will require a different type of fleece than a coarse floor rug.

My back aches when I have been sitting at the spinning wheel for some time. What causes this?

This is usually caused by the wrong posture or a chair that is the wrong height or shape. Do not crouch over the wheel in a tense position. Sit back and relax. Your back should be supported by the back of the chair, and it is also less tiring if your thighs are supported. Spin with your stationary hand resting in your lap where possible.

Most beginners have this problem as they are tense and not yet at ease with the whole process. A conscious effort to relax will help, and will also improve your spinning as your hands will not grip the wool as tightly, letting it flow freely.

Can I use commercial knitting patterns for my handspun yarn?

Yes. One method is to buy a ball of the wool specified in the pattern, and to spin a matching yarn. Tension samples will also be necessary. Cast on 20-30 stitches on the needle size stated in the pattern, and knit for 7cm (2-3in). Then change to larger-size needles, and continue knitting for another 7cm (2-3in). Change to a smaller size and knit for the same length before casting off. Wash and press the sample before making a judgment on the correct tension. Handspun wool should always be light and airy when knitted, so take this into account when selecting the tension. Count the stitches for 2.5cm (1in) on the sample that you feel is correct, and use this tension throughout the pattern.

I want to knit a strong, hardwearing, outdoor jersey. What do I do?

Spin a worsted yarn, using a medium to strong crossbred fleece such as a Romney or Border Leicester. Choose a knitting pattern with no lacy, open areas. A firm stitch, such as stocking stitch, would be suitable.

Can I prevent my handspun wool from shrinking?

Yes. Different types of fleece shrink more than others. As a general guideline, the finer the fleece, the more it will shrink. The wool can be pre-shrunk before knitting or weaving. Wash the skeins normally in warm soapy water, then dunk each skein in very hot water, and immediately in very cold water. Weighting the skein while drying will also help. Corriedale fleece is one that seems to have a propensity for shrinking and matting.

Fig. 7:1 Spinning posture

Can I wash a handspun jersey satisfactorily in the washing machine?

No. Even on the most gentle cycle the jersey will shrink and felt. Handwash, then put the jersey in the spin cycle to remove excess water.

A jersey I knitted recently, lost all the elasticity in the ribbed bands after just a couple of washes. I want to use the same fleece for another jersey. How can I prevent this happening again?

Some fleeces, particularly from the coarser breeds, have little elasticity. An excellent way to solve this problem is to buy some very fine elastic thread. This is so fine it is invisible when knitted along with your handspun yarn, in the ribbed areas.

My handspun yarn has a hairy surface, even though I carefully smooth the yarn when both spinning and plying. I feel a garment knitted with this wool will be rough and itchy to wear. What is wrong with my spinning?

It is not your spinning that is at fault, but the choice of fleece. A coarse, strong fleece, such as an English Leicester or Lincoln, is hairy and harsh to handle. Spinning it, however carefully, will not change these characteristics. Choose a fine, softer fleece next time.

Can I brush handspun wool to raise the surface?

Yes. Stretch the skein onto the niddy noddy or a revolving skeiner, and brush it firmly with a hairbrush dipped in hot water.

Is there any way I can improve the appearance of my yarn while I am plying. I have thick, slubby sections now and then, followed by thin places.

This uneven spinning will disappear with practice, but in the meantime careful plying will help. Watch the strands as you ply. When you get to a thick, slubby piece, let more twist than usual accumulate in this section. This will flatten the slub. In a thin area, hurry over this portion, with less twist than usual. This will bulk up these strands.

Should I spin all the yarn for a garment before I begin knitting.

Yes. It is tempting to spin some yarn, then knit; spin some more, and knit, and so on. Unless you are a very consistent spinner there will be variations in your spinning. Spin all the wool you think you will need and sort it before knitting. A slightly darker or thicker skein can be disguised in the ribbed bands.

How do I use a spindle?

Many spinners feel that the spindle should be mastered before a beginner spinner moves onto the wheel and it certainly does make learning to spin on a wheel easier. However, it can discourage the beginner who finds spindle spinning difficult, and he/she may give up in disgust and never try spinning on a wheel. Follow the step-by-step instructions below.

52a Attach a leader to the spindle as shown. First take the loose end under the whorl, to prevent the spun yarn from slipping off the shaft as the spindle is dropped. Then bring the leader up and out of the top groove.

52b Take a small piece of wool and hold it to the end of the leader with the left hand.

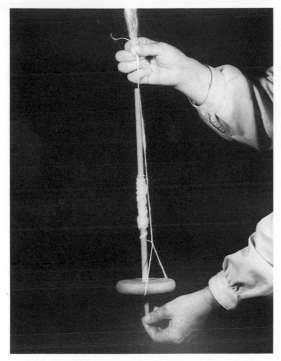

52c Twirl the spindle with the right hand in a clockwise direction.

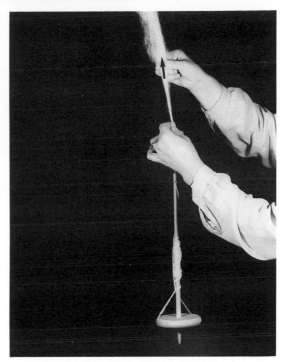

52d Draft the wool upwards with the right hand. The weight of the spindle will also help draft the fibres as it adds to the downwards pull. If the spindle stops rotating, twirl it again in the same direction.

Plying can be done on the spindle in the same manner as spinning, but it is more usual to spin only singles.

What type of wheel should I choose for my first spinning wheel?

A Traditional wheel is the usual choice for a beginner (see the Ashford Traditional, page 131). It has a drive ratio in the middle range, and will spin from fine/medium to medium/bulky yarns. The Scotch tension is easily understood and controlled by beginners.

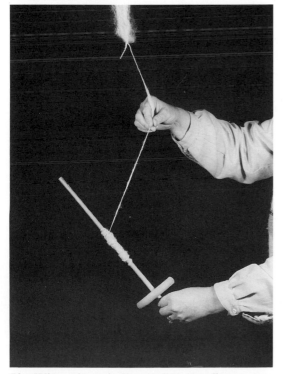

52e When the spindle reaches the floor, stop and wind the spun yarn onto the shaft.

CHAPTER EIGHT

Wool Dyeing

Plant dyeing · Wool preparation · Equipment · Mordants · Dyeing · Additives · Recipes · Lichens · Other dyestuffs · Chemical dyeing

PLANT DYEING

Many spinners find that dyeing their hand spun wool is a very creative and satisfying process. Plant dyeing seems to follow naturally from the craft of spinning and the range of colours is subtle and fitting for handspun wool. In this chapter I will introduce you to the subject, knowing full well that once you have begun this step to dyeing it is hard to stop. If you wish to explore this subject further, you will find many good books on the subject. (Some are listed in the Bibliography.)

One of the exciting things about plant dyeing, is that the colours will vary according to the season, climate, and the soil. This makes dyeing somewhat unpredictable, which all adds to the fun, as even the most experienced dyer will not be able to totally guarantee the colour that will emerge from the pot. Most of the plant dye colours blend well, as they do in nature, and there are few discordant shades and colours. A bag of mixed, plant-dyed wools is a joy to behold. Also the history behind each colour adds to the interest. A dyer may describe a colour as 'That was from the rhododendron collected when we were on holiday last year.'

Grey or light brown fleeces can be dyed. This adds another dimension to the colour range of plant dyeing, as the original fleece colour adds depth and subtlety to the colours.

WOOL PREPARATION

Spun and skeined wool
Wool must be thoroughly washed and scoured free of all grease. If the grease is left in the wool, the dye will not take evenly. Repeat the soaking, washing and rinsing procedure (described as the second method in Chapter One) several times. Use loose ties on the skein, to enable the soapy water, and later the dye, to penetrate well into the skein.

Fleece wool
Fleece wool or sliver can be dyed and then spun. Wash it carefully, as it must be free from grease. Interesting variations in dyeing fleece wool can occur. The tip of the staple is usually weathered, and will dye a deeper shade than the rest of the staple.

EQUIPMENT

Use a stainless steel or unchipped enamel pot with a lid, as these metals will not affect the dye. Do not use this pot for cooking because many dyes and chemicals are poisonous. You will also need a length of wooden dowelling or a glass rod to lift the skeins out of the dye pot, and an apron and rubber gloves to protect you from being dyed as well as the wool.

MORDANTS

A mordant is a substance that enables the wool to take up the dye and keep it. There are a few dyes which do not need mordants and these are called 'substantive' dyes. There are several mordants, and each will produce a different colour. The most common mordants are:

A. Alum (Potassium aluminium sulphate)
B. Chrome (Potassium dichromate)
C. Copper sulphate
D. Tin (Stannous chloride)

Some of these chemicals are poisonous so label them carefully and store them away from food. Take care in using chemicals. A mask can be worn to avoid breathing in the fumes; ensure adequate ventilation and avoid skin contact.

It is usual to mordant the wool before dyeing. Fill the dyepot with enough warm water to completely cover the wool when it is added later. Weigh the dry, scoured wool as this will tell you the correct quantities of mordant and plant material to use. Dissolve the mordant (plus the cream of tartar if this is included in the recipe — see Table 2), in hot water, and add to the pot, stirring well. Wet the scoured wool, thoroughly, add to the pot, and bring the pot to the boil. Simmer for ¾ to 1 hour. Do not stir the wool in the pot, or it will felt. Use the following table for amounts, results and information on each mordant. Note that fine wools require a smaller amount of mordant than strong wools.

TABLE 2

Mordant	ALUM	CHROME	COPPER SULPHATE	TIN
Recipe	85–115gm (3–4oz) of alum 28gm (1oz) cream of tartar 450gm (1lb) wool	7–14gm (¼–½oz) of chrome 450gm (1lb) wool	14gm (½oz) of copper sulphate 450gm (1lb) wool	14gm (½oz) tin 56gm (2oz) of cream of tartar 450gm (1lb) wool
When to Use	Store wet wool in dark cupboard for 2–3 days before dyeing	Can be used immediately but is better kept damp in a plastic bag for a few days (but not longer)	Immediately	As for chrome
Result of too much mordant	Wool will be sticky and harsh			Wool will be harsh and brittle
Effect on Colour		Darker, faster colours	Brings out green colours well	Brightens colours
General	If wool used immediately after mordanting, colour will be subdued. Most commonly used mordant.	Store chrome crystals in a dark bottle as they are sensitive to light. Poisonous, so handle carefully. Leaves wool soft and silky.	Can be added during dyeing.	Can be added during dyeing even if the wool has been treated with another mordant.

This is where the fun begins. You will need at least the same weight of plant material as wool. In the case of lighter materials, such as leaves, this will be a very large quantity, but in all cases be generous with the amount of plant material you gather. Soft-stalked plants such as mint, dahlias, flax seeds, or soft fruits and berries do not need pre-soaking to soften them, but hard dyestuff, such as bark or nuts, may need soaking for up to a week. The resulting water will be used as the base in the dye bath. If the plant material is likely to become entangled with the wool, as in the case of twigs or leaves, put it into a muslin bag before dyeing.

Remember not to put cold, wet wool into boiling water, or hot, wet wool into cold water. Use plenty of water in the dyepot as this will ensure that the dye is distributed evenly around the wool. A useful rule of thumb is no less than 1 litre of water for every 25 gm of wool.

There are two main methods of dyeing.

Method 1
Add the plant material to the correct amount of water (enough to completely cover the wool which will be added later). Slowly bring the water to just below the boil and simmer until all the dye has been extracted from the plant. Over-boiling will cause drab colours. Remove the plant material and stir well. Add the pre-mordanted wool, making sure it is thoroughly wet, and simmer until the desired colour is reached. Remember the wool will lighten in colour once it has dried. It is a great temptation to stir the wool in the dye pot, but this will cause felting. You can turn it gently once or twice. Hook the wool over a rod, slowly take it out of the water, and turn it over before replacing it in the pot. Remove the wool, rinse well and dry.

Method 2
The plant material and wool are heated together. This method is better for 'clean' plant material which will not become entangled in the wool. Put it and the wet pre-mordanted wool in the dyepot with enough water to completely cover the wool. Bring to the boil, simmer until the colour is correct, then remove the wool, rinse and dry.

With both methods, leaving the wool in the cooling dyebath overnight will deepen the colour, but may cause unevenness.

A third method has the wool, mixed mordant and plant material all placed in the dye pot together. This is suitable for slowly released dyes, such as flax seeds and gum leaves, but it can produce an uneven dye. It is a quick method for dyeing fleece.

DYEBATH ADDITIVES

Either acids or alkalis can be added to the dyebath to change the colour. When adding these substances, wait until the wool is dyed, remove it from the pot, add the acid or alkali, mix well, and put the wool back. Leave for five minutes, and then rinse as before. Sodium bicarbonate (baking soda) is a common alkali and vinegar is a common acid. Try these additives if you are disappointed with the colour. Half to one teaspoon is sufficient.

RECIPES FOR DYEING

Dahlia flowers (Oranges and red colours)
The darker flowers give a deeper dye colour. Pick the flower heads, gathering about five times the weight of flowers to wool, and use while fresh.

Method 1 Simmer the flower heads for 10–15 minutes. Remove, add wool and simmer for 10 minutes.
Method 2 Simmer flower heads and wool for ¾–1 hour.

The addition of bicarbonate of soda (baking soda) will change the colour dramatically.

Onion skins (Yellow to bronze colours)
Pre-soak the skins.
Method 1 Simmer the skins for 15–20 minutes. Remove, add wool, and simmer for a further 10–15 minutes.
Method 2 Simmer skins and wool for ¾–1 hour.

Silver dollar gum leaves and twigs (*Eucalyptus cinerea*) (Red colours — stronger colours in summer)
This needs no mordant. Pre-soak.
Method 1 Boil the twigs and leaves until the red dye is released (about 30 minutes). Remove the plant material, add the wool and simmer for 1 hour.
Method 2 Simmer the plant material and wool for about an hour.

Walnut shells (Browny-tan shades)
Choose walnut shells in the green, pickling stage. The wool does not need to be mordanted but this will give it a deeper colour. Pre-soak the shells for several days.
Method 1 Simmer the shells for 30–40 minutes, remove from the water, add the wool and simmer for 1 hour.

Method 2 Simmer the shells and wool for one and a half hours.

Some beautiful dye colours come from lichens. These are substantive dyes, needing no mordant. Be careful how you gather them: they are becoming scarce in some places, and take a long time to grow. Gather only small quantities and then only from places where they are plentiful. There are many types of lichens, each producing a variety of colours. Pre-soak them for at least 24 hours.
Method 1 Simmer the lichen for 2 hours, remove, add the wool and simmer for another 2 hours.
Method 2 Simmer the wool and lichen together for 2 hours.

Nearly all plant material will produce some colour, so experiment with your own garden plants. It can be really exciting, waiting to see what colour will come forth. Test your new colours for fading by putting a few strands half in, half out of a matchbox on a sunny window-sill. A few days of strong sunlight will soon test colour fastness.

Keep records of all your dyeing experiments — failures as well as successes. It is infuriating to forget how you came by a particularly good colour.

OTHER DYESTUFFS

Madder, woad, indigo, logwood, saffron and weld, are all traditional dye sources used around the world. Other plant materials you may like to experiment with are: French marigolds, asters, antirrhinum flowers, elderberries, wattle flowers and bark, and spindleberries.

CHEMICAL DYEING

A large industry has grown around the dyeing of fibres, and many of these dyes are now available to hand spinners. Many dyers buy the three primary colours, red, yellow and blue, and use these as a base for mixing all the other colours. Careful mixing of dyes is needed to produce interesting colours, and it is this lack of mixing that has led to many people thinking that chemical dyes are strong and artificial. This is the dyer's fault, not the dyes. It can be great fun mixing the dyes to get just the right shade. Some chemical dyes can be bought ready mixed to the colour you want, and if you do not want to experiment, these would be ideal.

Additional chemicals are needed, such as acetic acid, and levelling agents. Each dye manufacturer will have his own chemicals and instructions, which you should follow carefully for the best results. These dye kits can be bought from spinning supply shops. Dyes are developed for specific fibres. Many household dyes are marketed as 'union dyes', that is they contain the chemicals for both wool and cotton reactions. Check that the dye is suitable for the intended fibre.

Follow the washing instructions for wool at the beginning of this chapter, and use the same equipment as for plant dyeing. The wool will not need mordanting, as this chemical is included in the dyes or dye kit.

Take care in using chemical dyes, many have cancer-causing properties. Do not breathe the fumes, scatter powder, or allow the dye to come into contact with the skin. Ensure adequate ventilation, and do not use kitchen utensils in the dyeing process. Store dyestuffs safely away from children's reach.

CHAPTER NINE

Felting

Equipment · Fleece · Preparation of fleece · First project: making a ball. Second project: a sample piece.

Handmade felt is another product that can be made from fleece wool. It fits so well into the cycle of spinning, dyeing, knitting and weaving, that I feel it has a place in this book. Again, as with dyeing, I will provide just enough basic information to whet your appetite.

Felting is the process that, up until now, you have been trying to avoid. If three conditions — heat, moisture and movement — are present when wool is washed, felt is the result. We all know what happens to a woollen jersey when it has (accidentally, I hope) been through the complete cycle of the washing machine. The wool fibres shrink and mat together. This shrinking and matting, carried to extremes in controlled conditions, causes felt. Felt is a very strong, water-repellent fabric with an interesting surface texture. It can be used for boots,

mittens, hats, bags, garments such as waistcoats and jackets, and for decorative hangings and sculptures.

There are two methods of making felt articles. The article can be felted to fit the pattern shape, leaving no joins or seams. The other method is to felt a large piece, and then cut the article out of this piece, as you would with a dressmaking pattern. The latter method gives the article seams, which can be laced or embroidered together, and can add surface decoration to the piece. Both methods have a place, depending on the finished shape and end use of the article, so try both and see which you prefer.

In either case you will need soap powder or detergent, a plastic bowl, a piece of old sheeting and 2m (yds) of string or twine.

FLEECE

Each breed of sheep will felt differently. As a general rule, a fine fleece, closely-crimped, will felt better than a strong fleece with little crimp. Choice of fleece will also depend on the finished article. A pair of boots will require a strong, hardwearing fleece, and a soft waistcoat will

need a fine fleece. Choose a clean fleece, with little vegetable matter and discolouration. A tender fleece, with a break in it, will felt more easily than a sound fleece. If you choose a dirty old fleece that is hairy and rough, that is exactly how your piece of felt will look.

PREPARATION OF FLEECE

Wool is better carded before felting if smooth felt is required and either greasy or scoured wool can be used. The easiest method is probably to buy carded sliver, in which case all the preparation will have been done for you. If you do card your own wool, use either a

drumcarder, or handcarders as described in Chapter Three. Do not use flick carders or a comb, as this removes the short fibres necessary in felting. Always card more than you think you will need, as the wool disappears like magic during the felting process.

MAKING A BALL

This first sample project will help you understand what happens during felting. Take a handful of carded wool, pour over it a mixture of hot water (as hot as you can handle) and detergent. Soap powder can be used instead of detergent, but dissolve the powder well in the hot water first. Rub the wet wool between your hands to form a ball, and continue squeezing and rubbing until you have a solid ball of felt. It is surprising how much wool goes into a small ball. Experiment with layers of different colours of wool. Completely cover the entire ball with each felted colour, before adding the next layer. The ball can be cut to expose these layers. Rinse the ball in cold water, then hang out to dry.

A SAMPLE PIECE

It is wise to make a sample piece, before tackling specific articles. A sample will let you gauge how much wool is needed for a certain thickness of felt, and how much shrinkage will occur.

Take about 100–200gms (4–7oz), of carded wool, and divide it into three equal parts.

53a Spread one part over a dampened piece of sheeting 50cm (20in) square with all the fibres running left to right.

53b Spread the next portion over the first with the fibres running at right angles to the first layer.

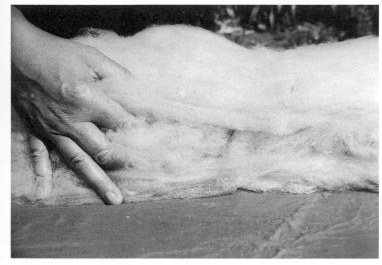

53c Spread the last portion with the fibres running left to right again.

53d Over these layers, pour a mixture of very hot water and detergent (1 litre to 2 table-spoons of detergent). Hot water and soap powder can be used in the same proportion. Thoroughly wet the wool all over.

53e Pat the wool for a few minutes, taking care not to move the fibres apart, until the fibres are beginning to felt.

53f Now rub the wool with a circular movement until the wool begins to solidify.

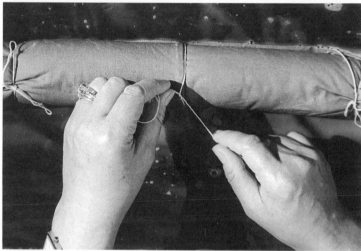

53g Roll the felt up in the sheet, tie it in two or three places. Roll it on the table, rather like rolling pastry for 5–10 minutes.

53h Undo the roll and re-roll at right angles to the original direction, and continue rolling.

53i Finished piece of felt.

How long the last stage takes will depend on how solid you want your felt to be, and how quick that particular fleece is to felt. When you have finished felting, hold the piece of felt up to the light. It should have no thin patches which let the light shine through. Rinse in cold water and hang out to dry.

There are many different ways of felt-making. An Ashford felting board or an old-fashioned corrugated washboard can be used instead of the rolling method I have described. A rather drastic method I heard of was when a large piece of felt was made by driving a truck back and forth over the piece! This would only be practical if you have a truck, a heavy traffic licence, and cheap petrol.

Practise felt-making until you are happy with the standard of your felt, and then begin making some finished pieces. Embroidery or crochet may add finishing touches to the articles, or small pieces of contrasting fleece can be felted to the surface to add interest. The surface decoration should look part of the piece and be a planned and integral part.

CHAPTER TEN

Patterns for Handspun Yarns

Knitting abbreviations • Old world-new style tabard • Cables for the outdoor man • Sweater: beginner's luck • Daisy pullover • Handwoven scarf • A shawl for all occasions • Houndstooth tabard • Tomboy sweater • Handspun baby's booties and slippers • Children's stretch hat and mittens • Toddler's jacket, hat and mittens • Fleece lampshade • Novelty yarn lampshade • Handwoven tablemats • Felt egg • Handwoven jacket fabric • Felt bag • Circular hanging • Felt hanging

There is nothing more exciting than knitting up your first skeins of handspun yarn. There is no doubt it will be an original yarn with an individual texture. No two spinners ever produce an identical yarn. In fact, for many of us, it takes lots of practice to spin large quantities of uniform yarn, and therefore it is not easy to design perfect patterns for handspuns. The patterns in this book have been created to help the beginner spinner and knitter or weaver achieve instant success.

The appeal of a handspun garment is the yarn itself, and these selected patterns reflect that aspect in their simple stitches and styling. Flexibility and adaptability are also keynotes of these garments. Small articles, such as hats, mittens, and slippers, are excellent projects on which to start.

For the most part you will doubtless be pleased with the yarn you have spun and look for a pattern to suit it. However, after more experience and practice, you will find it is possible to look first for a pattern and then spin the specified yarn. Because you are an enthusiastic spinner, creating your own original yarns, you will eventually want to create your own handknits and weaving patterns. The patterns in this book are easy to build on, adapt or modify. As a handspinner you are limited only by your imagination. So now, enjoy every aspect of spinning, confident that you are making something uniquely your own.

KNITTING ABBREVIATIONS

These save time and space in written patterns. They are easy to understand and quick to follow.

K.	knit	dec.	decrease	Ll	Pick up loop between sts and K. into loop
P.	purl	tog.	together		
st(s)	stitches	inc.	increase	Sl	slip
rem.	remaining	fwd.	forward	Pins	spare knitting needles or safety pins
stst	stocking stitch	beg.	begin	WPI	Wraps per inch (2.5cm) This means the number of wraps of yarn required to cover one inch (or 2.5cm) when wound around a ruler. For full explanation see p. 49

Old World – New Style Tabard

A tabard with a classical rounded neck to complement a blouse or shirt. Use small skeins from the dyepot and the easy-to-follow graphs below. See the photograph on p. 89.

Size: 87cm (34in) bust. An easy and flexible fit.

Actual measurements: Bust 92cm (36in); length centre back 61cm (24in).

Materials: Romney fleece wool spun in the grease to a medium weight 2-ply yarn.

300g medium handspun, approx. 13 WPI (2.5cm)

7 small skeins of coloured wool

1 stitch holder

1 darning needle

2 wooden buttons

1 pair 4.5mm (7) needles

Tension: Approx. 5 sts and 6 rows to 2.5cm (1in) in stst.

Back

Using 4.5mm needles cast on 81 sts in main colour. Knit 8 rows moss st. (1st row K.1, P.1. 2nd row K.1, P.1).

9th row: Work 6 sts moss st., knit to last 6 sts, moss st 6.

10th row: Work 6 sts moss st., purl to last 6 sts, moss st. 6.

continue this pattern until work measures 57cm (23in) or length required.

To shape shoulders: Cast off 8 sts at beginning of next 4 rows. Cast off 9 sts at the beginning of next 2 rows. Cast off remaining 31 sts.

Front

Work as for back until 10th row is completed. Repeat 9th and 10th rows. Follow instructions for pattern remembering to work 6 sts moss st on all edges.

Next row: K.4, join in gold (X) for beginning of graph 1. Continue on graph 1 for 4 rows.

Next row: with right side facing, continue in gold, then K.10 sts main colour and join green (O). Continue with graph 1 joining in white and then light brown as shown. When graph 1 is completed, knit in stst for 2 rows.

Next row: K.40, join in orange (–) and work graph 2 until completed.

Next row: K.60, join in lemon (s) and work graph 3 until angle of design is reached for beginning of neck opening.

To divide for front opening: Continue on graph 3, K.38 and place sts on holder. Continue across row, working 6 moss st to work neck opening. On 8th row make a button-hole at neck opening as follows: K.1, P.1, cast off 2, K.1, P.1. Next row: Cast on 2 sts over hole for button-hole.

When graph 3 is completed, cast off 10 sts at neck edge. Cast off 1st st on neck edge every alternate row until 25 sts remain. Continue length to match back.

Shoulders: Cast off 8 sts at beginning of armhole edge on next 2 rows.

Next row: cast off last 9 sts at beginning of armhole edge.

Rejoin wool at centre opening and cast on 6 sts. Work 1 row P. Next row: K.6, join in green (o) and continue on graph 4, keeping 6 sts in moss st at neck flap. Work other side of opening with reverse neck shaping. After completion of graph 4, K. 2 rows stst in main colour.

Next row: K.4 and join in white (/) and work graph 5. Work 6 rows stst.

Next row: K.2, join in rust for graph 6. Work four rows of graph 6 then join in light brown to complete it. Work reverse shaping for shoulder and cast off at armhole edge as above. Join shoulder seams.

Neck band

Pick up and knit 106 sts evenly around neck. continue band in moss st making button-hole on 2nd row as before. Cast off in rib after 6 rows have been worked.

To make up

Sew side seams, leaving a large opening for armhole and 13cm (5in) side vents. Sew on buttons — leather, wood or bone buttons enhance this garment.

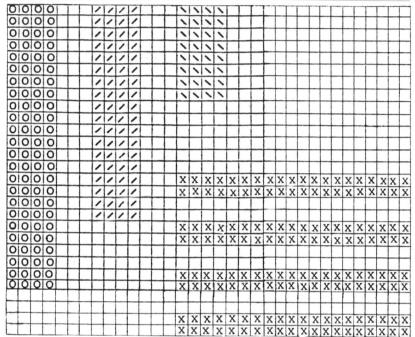

Graph 1

Instructions for knitting colour graphs

• Read graphs from lower right-hand side.
• Do not weave colours in fairisle pattern.
• Use separate small balls for each colour.
• When changing colours, twist the colour to be used underneath and to the right of the colour just used.
• When beginning a new colour, give a gentle tug to even-up loose tension.

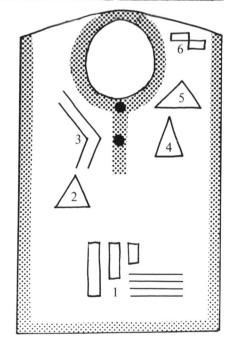

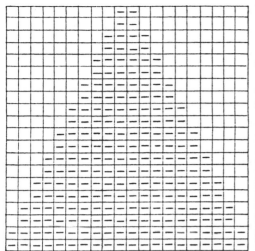

Graph 2

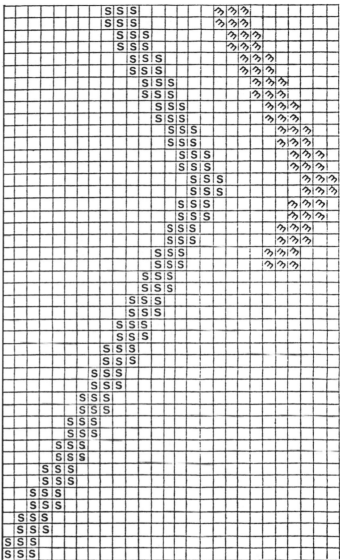

Graph 3

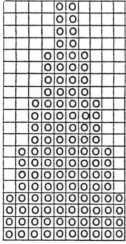 Rust	

Rust

Lemon

Gold

Green

White

Light Brown

Orange

Graph 4

Graph 5

Graph 6

Cables for the Outdoor Man

A warm and hard-wearing jersey with a very simple cable pattern.

Size: Actual measurements: chest 110cm (44in); length centre back 70cm (27½in).

A comfortable fit for approx. 104cm (41in) chest.

Materials: Grey, medium crossbred fleece, spun in 2-ply to standard triple knitting yarn

1.2kg handspun bulky, approx. 8/12 WPI (2.5cm)

1 heavy zip 24cm (9½in)

1 pair each size 5mm (6) and 4mm (8) needles

1 cable needle, pointed at both ends

Tension: Approx. 7 sts and 11 rows to 5cm (2in)

Back

With size 4mm needles cast on 101 sts and work in K.1, P.1 rib until work measures 7.5cm (3in), decreasing 1 st on last row. Change to 5mm needles and work pattern as follows:

1st row: K.11, P.3, * K.6, P.5, rep from * 5 times, K.6, P.3, K.11.

2nd row: P.11, K.3, * P.6, K.5, rep from * 5 times, P.6, K.3, P.11.

Repeat 1st and 2nd row once.

5th row: K.11, P.3, * slip next 3 sts on to cable needle and leave at front of work. K.3 sts, then K.3 sts from cable needle to form cable, P.5. Repeat from * 5 times, repeat cable once more, P.3, K.11.

6th row: Repeat 2nd row.

These six rows form the pattern. Repeat until work measures 44cm (17½in).

To shape armholes: Continue in pattern, but cast off 10 sts at beginning of next 2 rows. Work a further 12 rows in pattern. With right side facing, change to K.1, P.1 rib starting and ending with K.st. Continue ribbing for 40 rows in all.

To shape shoulders: Continue in rib, but cast off 8 sts at beginning of next 6 rows. Leave remaining 48 sts on spare needle.

Front

Work as for back until armhole decreases have been made. Continue in cable pattern for a further 6 rows (or first K. row after the next cable twist).

Divide for zip opening: K.1, P.3, (K.6, P.5, twice), K.6, (K.1, P.1, 3 times), K.1. Cast off 1 st (centre). Put remaining sts on spare needle. Turn and work on these 39 sts thus:

Rib 13 sts. Continue cable pattern across row. Next row: Work pattern for 15 sts, work to end in rib. Next row: Rib 30 sts, work in pattern to end of row. Next row: Work in rib. Continue in ribbing for 30 rows.

To shape neck: Continue in rib, slip 8 sts onto safety-pin (neck edge) and dec. 1 st at neck edge on the following 7 rows. Work 2 more rows without shaping.

To shape shoulder: Cast off 8 sts at shoulder edge on next 3 alternate rows. Return to sts on spare needle and work other side, but with reversed shapings. Commence ribbing at the zip edge with K.st.

Sleeves

Using 4mm needles, cast on 56 sts. Work 7.5cm (3in) in K.1, P.1 rib. Change to 5mm needles and work pattern as before.

1st row: P.3, (K.6, P.5, 4 times), K.6, P.3.

2nd row: K.3, (P.6, K.5, 4 times), P.6, K.3.

(Cont.)

Old world-new style tabard (*Wilma Wolfreys*) and a handsome cable sweater (*Evelyn O'Donnell*)

'Beginner's luck' (*Wilma Wolfreys*)

Repeat these two rows once.

5th row: Working in cable, increase 1st at each end of every 6th row. Continue to increase until there are 76 sts, then continue straight, working pattern, until work measures 57cm (22½in). Cast off loosely.

Neck

Join shoulder seams. With 5mm needles pick up 81 sts in continuous rib. Change to 4mm needles and work 30 rows. Cast off very loosely.

To make up

Sew in sleeves, matching patterns neatly. Sew up sleeve and body seams, and stitch in zip. Fold in neck ribbing and stitch loosely, allowing for stretch.

Sweater: Beginner's Luck

Front, back and two sleeves are four rectangles all the same size, knitted diagonally, starting and ending with 2 stitches. Use natural coloured Romney fleece in brown, grey and white, spun in a soft, light twist 2-ply bulky yarn, approximately 10 WPI (2.5cm).

Size: 81–86cm (32–34in) bust. Actual measurements 92cm (36in) bust; length centre back 50cm (20in)
Materials: 200g each of the 3 colours
Needles: 1 pair 4.5mm (7), 1 pair 8mm (0)
Tension: Approximately 3 stitches to 2.5cm (1in)

To knit rectangles

With 8mm needles cast on 2 sts in brown wool. Work in garter stitch, increasing at end of every row until 56 sts. Change to white wool and knit 10 rows as follows: Dec. at end of every odd row, but inc. at end of every even row. Change to grey wool and dec. at end of every row until all stitches are knitted off.
Knit three more identical rectangles.

Waist bands

Using 4.5mm needles, pick up 62 sts and knit in K.1 P.1 rib for 8cm (3in). Use large needles to cast off loosely in rib on all bands.

Sleeve bands

Using 4.5mm needles, pick up 32 sts and knit in K.1 P.1 rib for 8cm (3in). Cast off in rib.

Front neck edge:

Using 4.5mm needles, pick up 62 sts and knit in garter stitch for 10 rows. Cast off on wrong side.

Back neck edge

Using 4.5mm needles, pick up 62 sts and knit 1 row. Next row: K. to last 4 sts, turn. Next row: K. to last 8 sts, turn. Next row: K. to last 12 sts, turn. Next row: K. to end, then knit two rows. Cast off on wrong side.

To make up

Join at shoulder seam for 6cm (2½in). Fold sleeve in half widthwise and sew into place. Join sleeve and side seams.

Daisy Pullover

A flexible pullover pattern with no shapings and accent on the cuffs.

Size: To fit 86–91cm (34–36in) bust, loose fitting. Actual measurements: 104cm (40in) bust; 58cm (23in) length

Materials: A Romney fleece spun in the grease to a medium knitting yarn. 750g in 2-ply yarn. Approx. 15 WPI (2.5cm)
1 Pair size 4mm (8) needles

Tension: Approx. 5 stitches and 10 rows to 2.5cm (1in)

Front and back are knitted to the same pattern.
Using the thumb method, cast on 90 sts. Note the first row is the wrong side. Knit in garter stitch until work measures 41cm (16in) ending on wrong side. Mark each end of this row with coloured wool to indicate beginning of armhole. Continue in garter st. (Knit) for 73 rows. Cast off loosely.

Sleeves
Using the thumb method, cast on 79 sts. Work 3 rows in garter st. Work cuff pattern as follows:
1st row: *K.2, P.1, repeat from * to last st., K.1
2nd row: *P.2, K.1, repeat from * to last st., P.1
3rd row: *P.1, K.2, repeat from * to last st., P.1
4th row: *P.1, K.1, P.2, repeat from * to end
5th row: K.1, P.1, *K.2, P.1, repeat from * to last 2 sts. K.2
6th row: *K.1, P.2, repeat from * to last st., K.1
Repeat these 6 rows 3 times, then 1st row once, increasing 1 st at each end of row (wrong side facing).
Continue in garter st. (Knit) until work measures 43cm (17in). Cast off.

To make up
Join shoulder seams with a flat seam, leaving 25–30cm (10–12in) opening for neck. Join side seams up to coloured markers. Sew sleeve seams, reversing seam for turn-back cuff. Sew in sleeves. Press patterned cuff lightly and hold in position with a few catch stitches.

Handwoven Scarf

Spinning
Polwarth fleece. Yarn size: 21 wraps per 2.5cm (1in)

Weaving
Finished length: 130cm (51in)
Finished width: 20cm (8in)
Sett: 4 e.p.cm (10 e.p.i.)
Threading: Straight draw, 1,2,3,4
Weaving: Plain weave, 1 + 3, 2 + 4
Border patterns: Brooks Bouquet in a diamond shape
Finishing: Hemstitching
Weight: 80g (3oz)

Daisy pullover (*Mary Johnston*) and handwoven scarf (*spun and woven by the author*)

A shawl for all occasions (*Wilma Wolfreys*)

A Shawl for all Occasions

Knitted in three contrasting colours with matching fringing.

Size: 1.5m x 75cm (60 x 30in) without fringe

Materials: Soft and bulky handspun 2-ply Romney fleece wool, approximately 8/12 WPI (2.5cm). 150g brown, 150g grey, 60g white or three colours of your choice.

Needles: 10mm (000). If not available make your own needles from ⅜ inch dowelling.

Tension: 5 sts to 5cm (2in) on 10mm needles

Using brown wool cast on 4 sts.

1st row: K.1, wool fwd, k. to last stitch, wool fwd, K.1.

2nd row: knit.

These two rows make the pattern. Always change wool colour on first pattern row. Now continue in pattern as follows.

Knit 24 rows in brown
Knit 4 rows in white
Knit 2 rows in brown
Knit 4 rows in white
Knit 14 rows in grey
Knit 6 rows in brown
Knit 14 rows in grey
Knit 2 rows in white
Knit 2 rows in grey
Knit 2 rows in white
Knit 16 rows in brown
Knit 6 rows in white
Knit 4 rows in grey
Knit 2 rows in brown
Knit 2 rows in grey
Knit 2 rows in brown
Knit 4 rows in grey
Knit 2 rows in white
Knit 4 rows in brown
Knit 4 rows in grey (126 sts). Cast off.

8 strand fringe

Cut a piece of card 16cm (6½in) square. Wrap wool around four times. Cut at one end. Loop the folds (4) and knot through holes in edge of shawl, matching colours.

Houndstooth Tabard

Size: Actual measurements: bust 102cm (40in), centre back 53cm (21in).
Materials: Spun and knitted from Romney fleeces. 200g dark wool (A), 150g white wool (B), approx. 13 WPI (2.5cm)
1 pair size 3.75mm (9) and 4.5mm (7) needles
Stitch holder or safety pin
Tension: 5 sts to 2.5cm (1in).

Pattern
1st Row: With A, sl.1 purlwise, *K.2, sl.1 purlwise, repeat from * to end.
2nd row: P.
3rd row: With B, *K.2, sl.1 purlwise, repeat from * until 1 st remains, K.1.
4th row: P.
These 4 rows form the pattern.

Back
Using 3.75mm needles, cast on 100 sts in A and work in K.1, P.1 rib for 10cm (4in). Inc. 1 st at end of row (101 sts). Change to 4.5mm needles and work in pattern for 53cm (21in).

To shape shoulders: cast off 9 sts at beg. of next 6 rows. Cast off remaining 47 sts.

Front
Work as for back until work measures 44cm (17in). Keeping in pattern, K.40, place remaining sts on holder. Turn and continue to work in pattern, dec. 1 st. on neck edge every alternate row until 27 sts remain.

To shape shoulders: cast off 9 sts. at beg. of next 3 rows.
Leave centre 20 sts. on holder. Pick up remaining sts. and knit to correspond with other side.

Neck band: Join shoulder seams and using 3.75mm needles pick up and K.120 sts. evenly round neck. Work 6 rows K.1, P.1 rib. Cast off loosely in rib.

Armhole bands: Using 3.75mm needles, join in wool above waistband rib and pick up 126 sts (63 sts on each side of armhole). Work 6 rows K.1, P.1 rib. Cast off loosely.

To make up
Join side seams only on the waistbands. Now cross the front armbands over the back armbands plus 3 patterns of houndstooth. (This will give an overlap of approx. 6cm (2½in) at the top of the waistband). Sew the overlaps firmly in place.

Houndstooth tabard (*Wilma Wolfreys*)

Tomboy Sweater

Worked in fairisle on circular needles, following simple graphs.

Size: 56–61cm (22–24in) chest. Actual measurement: 67cm (26in); length 45cm (18in); sleeve seam 32cm (12½in).

Materials: Thick soft 2-ply handspun wool at approx. 9 WPI (2.5cm)
250g (8oz) grey (G) ☐
50g (2oz) brown (B) ▥
small quantity white (W) ☒
One each 60cm (24in) circular needle, sizes 5mm (6) and 6.5mm (3)
Safety pins or stitch holder
One set each of 4 needles pointed at both ends, sizes 5mm (6) and 6.5mm (3).
NOTE: Sets of 4 needles can be substituted for circular needles. A separate set of instructions is also included for sleeves done on 2 needles (size 6.5mm) if a set of 4 needles is unobtainable.

Tension: 15 sts to 10cm (4in) on 6.5mm (3) needles in stst.

Suggested cast-on method for maximum elasticity

1. Put a slip-loop on left needle.
2. Knit into loop and place second loop on to left needle.
3. Now purl between the two loops, ie, insert the right-hand needle from back to front between the loops, make a purl stitch and place the third loop on the left needle.
4. Knit between the last two loops and place the new loop on the left needle.
5. Continue alternately knitting and purling between loops until required number of stitches.

Continue to work in K.1, P.1 rib.

Back and front (knitted in the round)

Mark the beginning of each round with contrasting wool. Using 5mm circular needle cast on 84 sts in (B). Work 10 rounds in K.1, P.1 rib, increasing 12 sts evenly on last round (96 sts). Change to 6.5mm needle and using (W) for contrast, work 8 rows of chart 1. Change to (G) and work in stst until work measures 32cm (12½in) or length required.

Divide for armhole: Next round: K.20, place next 7 sts on to safety pin, K.41, place next 7 sts on safety pin, K. to end. Leave work while knitting sleeves.

OR if knitting sleeves on two needles, K.20, cast off next 7 sts, K.41, cast off next 7 sts, K. to end. Leave work while knitting sleeves.

Sleeves

Using set of four 5mm (6) needles and (B) cast on 24 sts. Mark end of each round with contrasting wool. Work 10 rounds in K.1, P.1 rib. Change to set of 6.5mm (3) needles and continuing in (B) follow 8 rows of chart 1 (using (W) for contrast). Change to (G) and work one round stst, then inc. 1 st at beg. and end of next and every following 8th round (32 sts). Continue without shaping until work measures 32cm (12½in) from cast-on edge (or length required).

Divide for armhole: Next round: K.3, place these sts on to spare pin, K.26, place last 3 sts on to spare pin and leave.

OR if using two needles —

Tomboy sweater (*Cindy Begg*) and felt bag (*Robyn Henderson*)

Chart 1

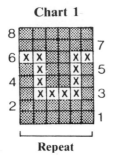

Repeat

Chart 2

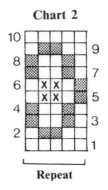

Repeat

Chart 3

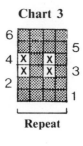

Repeat

Using 5mm (6) needles and (B) cast on 24 sts. K.10 rows in K.1, P.1 rib. Change to 6.5mm (3) needles and work 8 rows of chart 1 (using (W) for contrast). Change to (G) and work in stst. Inc. 1 st at beg. and end of next and every following 8th row (32 sts). Continue without shaping until work measures 31cm (12½in) or length required.

Armhole shaping: Place next 3 sts on to spare pin, K.26, place last 3 sts on spare pin. OR cast off 3 sts at beg. of next 2 rows.

Yoke

Place sts for yoke on to 60cm (24in) circular needle size 6.5mm (3) as follows: 20 sts from left back; 26 sts from left sleeve; 41 sts from front; 26 sts from right sleeve; 21 sts from right back (134 sts).
K.1 round in (G) and dec. 2 sts evenly (132 sts). Join in (B) and work rows 1–7 inclusive from chart 1.
Next round: (Dec. round) Still using (B), dec. by knitting 3rd and 4th sts tog., then every following 5th and 6th sts tog., ending with K.2 (110 sts).
K. one round in (G). Work rows 1–10 from chart 2.
Next round: (Dec. round) Using (G) dec. by knitting 2nd and 3rd sts tog., then every following 4th and 5th sts tog., ending with K.2 (88 sts). Using (B) work rows 1–5 inclusive from chart 3.
Next round: (Dec. round) Using (B) dec. by knitting 2nd and 3rd sts tog., then every following 3rd and 4th sts tog., ending with K.1 (66 sts). K. one round with (G).
Next round: (Dec. round) Using (G), dec. by knitting 1st and 2nd sts tog., then every following 2nd and 3rd sts tog., ending with K.1 (44 sts).

Neck band

Using set of four 5mm (6) needles and (B) work 16 rounds in K.1, P.1 rib. Cast off loosely in rib.

To make up

Join sts under arm by grafting sts tog. or sewing. Fold neckband in half to wrong side and slip stitch into position loosely. If sleeves were knitted on 2 needles, sew up seam.

Handspun Baby's Booties and Slippers

Although woolly sheepskin soles are used in these patterns, any suitable material may be substituted, e.g. handmade felt, leather, fur fabric, etc. These are excellent projects for using up small lots of left-over handspun and/or dyed yarn.

KNITTED GARTER STITCH BOOTIES

Materials: Romney yarn 90 per cent blend with 10 per cent mohair, approx. 18 WPI (2.5cm)
1 pair size 3.5mm (10) needles
Size: To fit 11cm (4½in) sole

With 3.5mm (10) needles cast on 65 sts and work 10 rows in garter st.
Begin instep shaping.
1st row: K.37, K.2 tog. tbs., turn.
2nd row: Sl.1, K.9, K.2 tog. turn.
3rd row: Sl.1, K.9, K.2 tog. tbs, turn.
Repeat these last two rows until 45 sts remain (17 sts at each side of instep shaping).
Sl.1, K.9, K.2 tog tbs., K. to end (44 sts).
Next row: K.

To make ribbon holes: K.1, *M.1, K.2 tog. Repeat from * until 1 st. K.1.
Work 11 rows in garter st. Cast off.
Join back seam and stitch to sole. Thread with ribbon or crocheted chain.

SLIPPERS

Materials: Grey fleece, medium to strong, approx. 8/10 WPI (2.5cm) 8 ply, spun as a 2-ply or a thick singles.
Sizes: To fit 11cm (4½in), 14cm (5½in), 17cm (6¾in) sole.

Using size 3.5mm (10) needles, cast on 10 (12,15) sts.
1st row: Sl.1, K. to end.
Repeat first row until work measures 12 (15, 20) cm.
Next row: Sl.1, K.9 (11, 14) sts, fold work in half and pick up 10 (12, 15) sts from cast-on edge (20, 24, 30 sts).
Next row: K. increasing 3 sts evenly across row (23, 27, 33 sts).
Next row: K.
Next row: Rib in K.1, P.1 to end. Repeat last row until work measures 5 (7, 8) cm.
Next row: K.1, K.2 tog. to end of row.
Next row: P.1, P.2 tog. to end of row.
Next row: K.1, K.2 tog. to end of row. Break yarn and thread through remaining sts, draw up tightly and fasten off. Stitch to sole and attach pompom to top of slipper.

A POMPOM

Use for hats and slippers, or make extra big one for a baby's ball.
Use stiff cardboard and cut two circles with the same diameter as the required pompom. Cut a small circle out of the centre of each. Hold the two shapes together and wind the yarn through the centre hole and spread evenly at the outer edge. When the centre hole is full, cut the loops at outer edge. Wind a strong thread between the two cardboard shapes and tie tightly. Remove the cardboard and trim pompom if necessary.

Abbreviations

ch.   chain
tr.   treble
sl.st.   slip stitch
d.c.   double crochet
dble tr. double treble
crab st. double crochet into double crochet of previous row, working from left to right

For American readers	
double crochet	= single crochet
treble	= double crochet
double treble	= treble

MOCCASINS

Materials

The thickness of the yarn is not vital. Hand-carded 90 per cent Romney and 10 per cent mohair, approx. 20 WPI (2.5cm) 4-ply
1 pair sheepskin soles 11cm (4½in); 14cm (5½in); 17cm (6¾in)
Size 3.50 crochet hook
2 small buttons (if ankle strap required)

Rosette or top

Make 6 ch., join into a ring with a sl.st.
1st row: 2 ch., work 15 tr. into ring, sl.st. to join into 2nd of first 2 ch.
2nd row: 3 ch. (1 tr. 1 ch.) 15 times, sl.st. to end of last 3 ch.
3rd row, 1st and 2nd sizes: 1 ch. *(1 dc. into space, 1 dc. into top of next tr.) 4 times, (1 tr. into space, 1 tr. into top of next tr.) 4 times*.
Repeat from * to * once. Sl.st. to 1st ch. Fasten off.
3rd row, 3rd size: 4 ch. (1 tr. 2 ch.) 15 times, sl.st. to 2nd of 4 ch.
4th row: 1 ch. *(2 dc. into space, 1 dc. into top of next tr.) 4 times, (2 tr. into space, 1 tr. into top of next tr.) 4 times*. Repeat from * to * once. Sl.st. to 1st ch. Fasten off.

Side

Mark centre toe and heel. With woolly side facing away from you, begin at hole left centre of heel. Work (1 dc. 1 ch.) twice into each hole, join with sl.st.
1st row: 3 ch. 1 tr. into each space until 2 tr. from centre toe, 2 tr. into next space, 1 tr., 2 tr. into next space, 1 tr. into each space until centre heel, 2 tr. into next space, join with sl.st. to top of 3 ch.
2nd row: 4 ch. 1 dble tr. into next 3 (4) (5) tr., 1 tr. into each tr. until 2 tr. from centre toe, 2 tr. into next tr., 1 tr., 2 tr. into next tr., 1 tr. into each tr. until 4 (5) (6) from centre heel, 1 dble tr. into next 4 (5) (6) tr. Join with a sl.st.
3rd row, 1st and 2nd sizes: 4 ch., 1 dble tr. into next 3 (4) tr., 1 tr., into each tr. until 4 (5) tr from centre heel, 1 dble tr into next 4 (5) tr. Join with sl.st.
3rd row, 3rd size: Same as 2nd row.
4th row, 1st and 2nd sizes: 1 ch., 1 dc. into each tr. until 12 tr. from centre toe, join in top (rosette fits lengthwise) by (dc. 1 tr. and 1 dc. from top together) 24 times, 1 dc. into each tr. across top of foot, sl.st. to side, 1 ch., crab st. across top of foot, 1 dc. into each tr. at side, join with sl.st. Crab st. around top of moccasin and fasten off.
4th row, 3rd size: 4ch. 1 dble tr. into next 5 tr., 1 tr. into each tr. until 6 tr. from centre heel, 1 dble tr. into next 6 tr., join with sl.st.
5th row: 1 ch., 1 dc. into each tr. until 18 tr. from centre toe, join in top by (dc. tr. and 1 dc. from top together) 36 times, 1 dc. into each tr. across top of foot, sl.st. to side, 1 ch., crab st. across top of foot, 1 dc. into each tr. at side, join with a sl.st. Crab st. around top of moccasin, fasten off.

Ankle strap

If required, an ankle strap may be made by making 50 (55) (60) ch., 1 dc. into 2nd chain from hook, 1 dc. 2 ch. 1 dc. into each chain to end. Fasten off.

Moccasins, lower right; crocheted booties, lower left; garter stitch booties, centre left; slippers, top (*Jill Hildyard*)

CROCHETED BABY'S BOOTIES

Materials: Medium wool blended with 10 per cent mohair hand-carded, approx. 11/16
WPI (2.5cm)
Small ball of yarn for working instep.
Size: To fit 11cm (4½in) sole.

With woolly side facing away from you and using no. 3.5mm crochet hook, begin
at centre heel and work (1 dc. 1 ch.) twice into each hole, join with a sl.st., turn.
Next row: 3 ch. 1 tr. into each space to end, join with a sl.st. in 3 ch., turn.
Next row: Repeat last row once into top of each tr. Draw loop on hook up to a height
of approx. 3cm (1¼in) to prevent unravelling, then remove hook from loop.

To shape instep: With woolly side facing you and using reserved yarn, miss first 18
tr., join yarn with sl.st. in next tr., miss 1 tr., 1 tr. into each of next 7 tr., sl.st across
next 2 tr., turn.
Next row: Miss 2 sl.sts., 1 tr. in each of next 7 tr., miss 2 tr., sl.st. across next 2
tr., turn. Repeat this row once more.
Next row: Miss 2 sl.sts., 1 tr. in each of next 7 tr., miss 1 tr., sl.st. into next tr.,
fasten off.
Return to main work.

Next row: With woolly side facing you work 3 ch., 1 tr. into each tr., sl.st. to 3 ch.
turn. Repeat this row 3 times, turn. Crab st. around top of bootie, fasten off. Thread
with ribbon or crocheted chain.

Children's stretch hat and mittens (*Joan Quigley*)

Children's Stretch Hat and Mittens

A quick project using small skeins of wool from experimental dyepots.

Sizes: To fit 2–4 years, 5–7 years, 8–10+ years.

Materials: Fleece wool: Coopworth and Borderdale spun to a 2-ply medium knitting yarn. Approx. 110g (main colour) 2-ply 15/20 WPI (2.5cm), plus contrast colours for stripes, approx. 15g
3½mm (10) and 4mm (8) knitting needles

Tension: 7 sts and 8 rows to 2.5cm (1in) in stst

HAT

Using main colour and 4mm needles, cast on 80 (88, 96) sts. Knit 8 (9, 10)cm in K.2, P.2 rib. Work 4 stripes in contrast. First row K., then 3 rows K.2, P.2 rib (for each colour). Join main colour, K.1 row, continue to work in K.2, P.2 rib until work measures 19 (20, 21)cm. Next row: K. 2 tog. to end of row. Knit 7 rows stst. Next row: K.2 tog. to end of row. Knit 5 rows stst. Last row: K.2 tog. to end of row. Break off yarn and draw through remaining sts. Sew seam. Make pompom and attach to hat.

MITTENS

Using 3½mm needles and first contrast colour cast on 32 (36, 40) sts. Work 4 rows in K.2, P.2 rib. Work four stripes altogether as for hat. Join main colour. For 2nd and 3rd sizes work a further 4 rows. Change to 4mm needles and work 8 (6, 8) rows in stst.

To increase for thumb: K.16 (18, 20), L1, K.2, L1, K.14 (16, 18).

Next row: P.

Next row: K.16 (18, 20), L1, K4, L1, K14 (16, 18).

Next row: P.

Next row: K.16 (18, 20), L1, K.6, L1, K.14 (16, 18).

Next row: P.

Next row: K.16 (18, 20), L1, K.8, L1, K.14 (16, 18).

Next row: P.

Next row: K.16 (18, 20), L1, K.10, L1, K.14 (16, 18).

Next row: P.

Next row: K.16 (18, 20) and carry on for thumb. Inc. into first st., K.10, inc., K.1. Continue on these 14 sts and work 9 (11, 13) rows stst.

Next row: K.2 tog. to end of row. Break off yarn and draw through remaining sts. Rejoin wool to continue with sts. on left hand needle. Inc. 1, K. to end of row. Continue in stst until work measures 16 (18, 20) cm.

Next row: K.1, *K.2 tog., K.2, repeat from * to last 2 sts, K.2 tog.

Next row: P.

Next row: K.2 tog., K.1, repeat to last 2 sts, K.2 tog.

Next row: P.

Next row: K.1, *K.2 tog., repeat from * to end of row. Break off yarn and draw through remaining sts.

Finished length 18 (20, 22) cm.

Make other mitten the same but reversing the thumb shapings. Sew down all seams and press mittens under a damp cloth.

Toddler's Jacket, Hat and Mittens

JACKET

This garment is knitted in one piece from Romney fleece spun in the grease to produce a medium bulky 2-ply yarn.

Size: To fit toddler 18–24 months. Actual measurements: chest 60cm (23½in); length centre back 30cm (12in).

Materials: 225g softly spun 2-ply yarn (includes 50g contrast colour, plant-dyed with beetroot). Approximately 10/12 WPI (2.5cm)
1 pair size 5.5mm (5) needles
4 buttons
Safety pin

Tension: Approximately 4 sts to 2.5cm (1in)

Back

Using main colour, cast on 48 sts. Join contrast and knit 2 rows. Next row: K. main colour. Next rows: K.2, P.2 for 7 rows. Continue in stocking stitch for 40 rows. Next row: cast on 30 sts for first sleeve, knit to end. Turn and cast on 30 sts for second sleeve (108 sts). Continue in stocking stitch for 17 rows.
To divide stitches for neck: next row K.47, turn and work on these sts for right front, leaving remaining stitches on holder.

Right front

Continue on 47 sts and work 15 rows stocking stitch. Next row: K. to end, turn and cast on 4 sts for neck (51 sts). Continue in stocking stitch for 5 rows. Next row: cast off 30 sts for sleeve, knit to end (21 sts). Continue in stocking stitch for 39 rows. Work 7 rows in K.2, P.2 rib. Next row: with right side facing, K.2 rows contrast. Knit 1 row main colour, cast off in main colour.

Left Front

With right side facing, join wool to inner end of stitches on spare needle. Cast off 14 sts and knit to end (47 sts). Work 15 rows stocking stitch. Next row: cast on 4 sts for neck, K. to end. Work 4 rows stocking stitch. Next row: cast off 30 sts for sleeve, P. to end (21 sts). Work 40 rows stocking stitch. Work 6 rows K.2, P.2 rib. With right side facing knit 2 rows in contrast. Knit 1 row in main colour and cast off.

Cuffs

Pick up 24 sts and work in K.2 P.2 rib for 5 rows. Knit 2 rows in contrast. Knit 1 row main colour and cast off.

Buttonhole band

With right side facing pick up and knit 40 sts. Work 3 rows in K.2 P.2 rib. With right side facing work first buttonhole. Rib 2 * cast off 2 sts, rib 9. Repeat from * twice. Cast off 2, rib 3 sts. Next row: work in rib, casting on 2 sts over those cast off in previous row. Knit 2 rows contrast, 1 row main and cast off.

Button band

Pick up and knit 40 sts and work as for buttonhole band but omit buttonholes.

Neckband

Pick up and knit 50 sts. Cast off 6 sts at beginning of next 2 rows. Next row: K.2 P.2 until 2 sts remain, turn and rib until 2 sts remain. Turn and rib until 4 sts remain,

Toddler's jacket, hat and mittens (*Wilma Wolfreys*)

turn and rib until 4 sts remain. Turn and rib until 6 sts remain, turn and rib until 6 sts remain. Slip these 6 sts on to needle so that all 38 sts are on needle, knit 2 rows in contrast. Knit 1 row in main colour and cast off.
Sew up seams and sew on buttons.

HAT

Cast on 60 sts in main colour. Join contrast and knit 2 rows. Knit 1 row main colour, then work 30 rows in K.2 P.2 rib. With wrong side facing K.2, K.2 tog. to end (45 sts). Purl 1 row. Next row: K.2 tog. K.1 to end (30 sts). Purl 1 row. Next row: K.2 tog. to end (15 sts).

   With a darning needle, thread through these stitches and sew seam leaving 5cm. Finish sewing on the other side for a neat turn-up.

MITTENS

Cast on 24 sts in main colour. Join in contrast and knit 2 rows. Change to main colour and knit 1 row. Work 6 rows in K.2 P.2 rib. With right side facing K.11 sts and increase into next 2 sts, K.11. Next row: purl. Next row: K.11, increase into next st. K.2. inc. into next st. K.11. Next row, purl. Continue increasing in the same way until there are 8 sts for thumb. Next row: k.12, put next 8 sts on spare pin. Cast on 2 sts and knit remaining 12 sts (26 sts). Work 7 rows in stocking stitch. Next row: K.2, K.2 tog. to last 2 stitches, K.2 (20 sts). Next row: purl. Next row: K.1, K.2 tog. to last 2 stitches, K.2 (14 sts). Next row: purl. Take a darning needle and thread wool through these stitches and sew seam.

Thumb
Pick up 8 sts from pin-holder and cast on 2 sts (10 sts). Work 4 rows in stocking stitch. Next row: K.2 tog. along row (5 sts). Purl 1 row, then thread wool through stitches with a darning needle and sew thumb, attaching the 2 cast-on stitches to the 2 cast on at the base of the thumb.

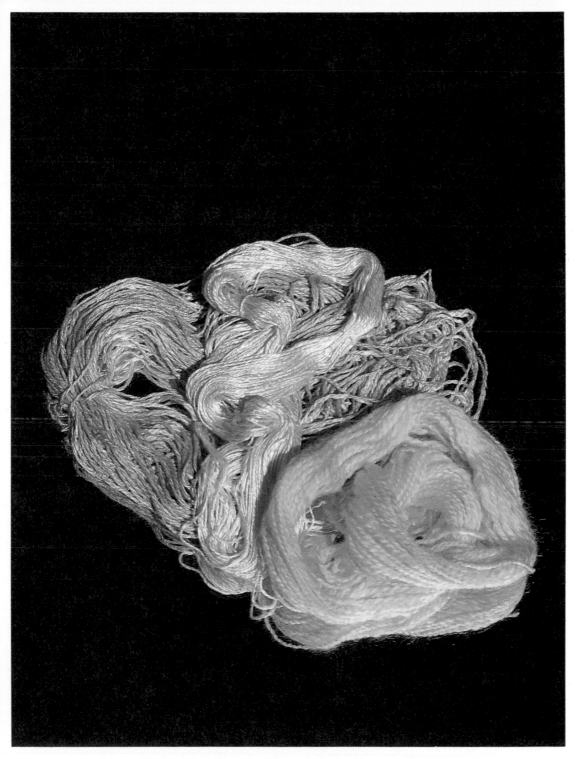

Skeins of spun Tussah silk, Ching Chiang silk and Romney wool

Fleece lampshade, left, and novelty yarn lampshade (*Gwen Fox*). Natural dyed fleece wool and handspun yarn (*Marian Gilbert*). The colours were achieved by using the following natural dyes and mordants: dark orange — dahlia flowers and alum; light orange — dahlia flowers and alum; pale yellow — eucalyptus and chrome; tan — walnuts, no mordant; yellowy green — rosemary and chrome; green — chrysanthemum and iron; medium brown — onion skins and tin; black — silver dollar gum and iron.

Fleece Lampshade

Requirements
Frame: A drum, tapered drum, chimney or coolee frame is preferable for ease of handling.
Carded fleece: This should be scoured and/or dyed to the desired colour. The fleece should be free of short, broken pieces. If plant-dyed wool is used, check that it is colour-fast, as it is disappointing if the colours fade. Chemical dyes are more reliable for lasting beauty. The lampshade illustrated was dyed with onion skins and green walnut shells.
Bouclé or novelty yarn

Binding the frame
From the side of a sliver of carded fleece in the main colour, peel a 'ribbon' approximately 2cm (¾in) wide, and slightly longer than the vertical wires. Keeping it flat, begin binding each vertical wire firmly, starting with a half-hitch around the top ring, and binding in the free end. End with a half-hitch around the lower ring, leaving a 3cm (1in) tail which will be covered later. Bind top and lower rings in a similar fashion.

Covering the frame
The next stage will be easier if the frame is fastened loosely to the lamp-base. Starting at the lower edge, place lengths of carded fleece around the frame, working towards the top. Attach each piece with a spring clothes-peg to the wires to facilitate handling.

If the frame is covered with one colour first, then other colours may be laid on in small pieces at intervals, e.g. brown on apricot, with small amounts of white for highlights.

A matching bouclé thread makes a good finish when wrapping and enclosing the fleece, but any novelty yarn can be used. A small ball of yarn is easier to handle. Tie the end to the lower ring, and work around the frame, going up and over, with regular spacing, 2½–3cm (1–1¼ins) apart at the lower edge. There should also be a thread over each vertical wire.

To complete, use a fine knitting needle to gently re-arrange the fleece where it may be thinner in some places.

Novelty Yarn Lampshade

Requirements
As for fleece lampshade.

Binding the frame
Bind the frame as for the fleece lampshade, using coloured, carded wool that will match the bouclé thread.

Bouclé yarn
Threads 1 and 2 are spun from the same dyed fleece used in the binding. The lampshade illustrated was dyed with dahlia flowers (chrome mordant). Three single threads are used to spin this novelty yarn.
1. *Loop thread* Spin a medium yarn from a strong fleece such as an English Leicester, with a Z-twist, and a worsted spinning method.
2. *Core thread* Spin an S-spun, fine, firmly-twisted yarn.
3. *Binder* Matching terylene sewing thread.

Take threads 1 and 2, the loop and the core threads. Place each bobbin of yarn onto a Lazy Kate, and place the Lazy Kates at each side of your spinning chair. Ply the singles together, with an S-twist, pushing the loop thread up as you do so. The loops can be as large or as small as you wish. With the Lazy Kates separated, it is easier to control the threads.

Place thread 3, the sewing thread, and the plyed yarn onto a Lazy Kate, and ply them together with a Z-twist. This binder thread can be plyed quickly, and will hold the loops in place.

Wrap the lampshade with this yarn in the same manner as when wrapping the fleece lampshade.

Handwoven Tablemats

Spinning
Yarn size: 12 wraps per 2.5cm (1in).

Dyeing
Yarns dyed with Weld, Eucalyptus, Carrot tops, Onion skins, African Marigolds, Walnuts, Dahlias, and Rosemary.

Weaving
Finished length: 34cm (13½in).
finished width: 28cm (11in).
Sett: 3 e.p.cm. (8 e.p.i.).
Threading: Straight draw, 1 2 3 4.
Weaving: reversible cord weave. 2 + 3, 2 + 4, 2 + 3, 1 + 3.
Finishing: Hemstitching.
Weight: 69g (2oz) each mat.

Felt Egg

The smallest ball that will form the yolk of the egg is felted first. Wrap this ball in fine, clinging, plastic film then cover this ball with more carded wool, in an appropriate colour. Felt this second ball. Repeat the plastic wrapping and felting until the desired size is reached. Cut through the ball, with a very sharp knife, to reveal the layers, and dry. While drying, it is best to keep the sections inside one another, as they will keep to the desired shape.

Handwoven table mats (*spun and dyed by Marian Gilbert*). Felt egg (*Jill Dando*)

Handwoven Jacket Fabric

Spinning
Yarn size: 11 wraps per 2.5cm (1in). singles.
Blended on carders. (See Chapter Three for blending.)

Weaving
Sett: 3 e.p.cm. (8 e.p.i.)
Threading: Straight draw, 1,2,3,4.
Weaving: Swiss twill, 1 + 2, 2 +3, 3 +4, 4.
Warp: 2 ply Wadsworth yarn, grey.
Weft: Handspun singles.

Felt Bag

See the photograph on p. 99.

Materials
Carded wool
Slivers of dyed wool tops
Piece of sheeting

Step 1
Wet a piece of sheeting or cotton, and smooth it onto a flat surface.

Step 2
Lay out the small slivers of dyed wool tops (in reverse) onto the sheeting to form the design.

Step 3
Lay the carded wool batt over the design, as explained in Chapter Nine, with three layers in opposite directions.

Step 4
Place a piece of sheeting or cotton cloth, shaped to the bag outline, but smaller than the batt, over the batt.

Step 5
Lay another batt of carded wool over the sheeting. The end result will resemble a sandwich of carded wool, with the sheeting as the filling.

Step 6
Wrap the sandwich in the dampened sheeting, and felt it, following the directions in Chapter Nine again.

Step 7
When felting is complete, remove the central piece of sheeting, and this leaves the bag opening.

Step 8
A handle of twisted wool adds the finishing touch.

Handwoven jacket fabric (*Spun by Irene van der Krogt, woven by the author*)

Circular Hanging

An off-loom weaving.

Materials
Small skeins of handspun wool.

Step 1
A. Buttonhole around the hoop, with stitches pushed tightly together.
B. Turn the edge to the centre.

Step 2
Put in the crossbars, catching the thread through buttonhole loops, in one of the following ways:
A. Vertical or horizontal — evenly or unevenly spaced.
B. Evenly spaced around the circle.
C. Unevenly spaced around the circle.
D. Abstract, i.e. any angles.

Step 3
Formation of designs. Take groups or bars and:
A. Bind over and over.
B. Buttonhole together.
C. Weave in and out.
D. Make spiderwebs.
E. Knot bars together with a twisted chain stitch.
F. Tease wool and weave through bars.

Note: All stitches can be close together or spread for different effects. Combinations of techniques give interesting results. Extra bars can be added into the weaving. Experiment — have fun!

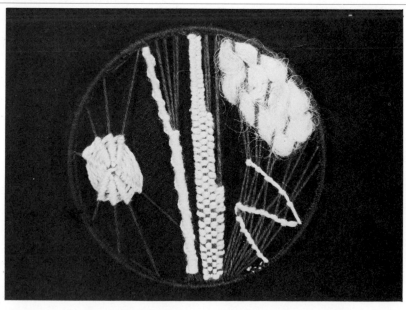

Circular wall hanging (*Barbara Bevis*)

Felt Hanging

The carded batts used for this hanging were made from commercially-dyed wool tops. However, you can dye your own wool, with either chemical or plant dyes. The background piece was felted in the usual manner. The curved pieces were first felted, and then rolled over a bottle and steamed to set the shape. *(Jill Dando)*

Plant-dyed skeins using onion skins, eucalyptus, chrysanthemums, dahlias, rosemary, silver dollar gum, and walnuts. (*Spun and dyed by Marian Gilbert*)

APPENDIX A:
SHEEP BREEDS AND WOOLS

CHARACTERISTICS OF NEW ZEALAND BREED WOOLS

Class	Breed	Micron	Qual. No.	Staple length (mm)	General characteristics	Notes on Spinning	Finished articles
Merino	Merino	23–19	60s–70s	75	Close crimp spacing. Soft, white wool, with firm staples. Flat tip.	Experience needed to spin this wool. Spin a very fine yarn.	Evening stoles, shawls, and baby wear.
Quarterbred	Polwarth	26–21	58s–64s	100	Soft wool, with a staple that is longer than Merino.	Fine spinning. Not as difficult as Merino, but not for beginners.	As above.
Halfbred	Corriedale	33–26	50s–58s	110	Moderately soft, with a compact, even crimp. Firm staple, which has a flat, somewhat matted tip.	Fine-medium spinning. Will bulk when washed. Elastic yarn, which felts easily.	Baby wear, woven, knitted and crocheted garments.
	Halfbred	33–26	50s–58s	110	As above	As above	As above
Fine crossbred	Perendale crossbred	35–28	48s–56s	125	Crisp-handling wool	Medium spinning. Excellent for beginners.	All purpose wool, for knitted, crocheted, and woven garments, curtains, upholstery, and fabrics.
	Borderdale	35–29	48s–54s	125	Firm staple, with a pointed tip.	As above	As above
	Romney	38–31	44s–52s	145	Staple less firm and more open, with oval tip. Buttery colour.	Medium spinning. Good for beginners.	As above
	Coopworth	38–33	44s–50s	150	Firm staple, more lustrous than Romney.	As above	As above
Medium crossbred	Perendale	35–28	48s–56s	125	As above	As above	Outdoor knitted, crocheted garments.
	Romney	38–31	44s–52s	145	As above	As above	Tweed-type fabrics. Wall hangings.
	Coopworth	38–33	44s–50s	150	As above	As above	Upholstery.
	Border Leicester	38–37	44s–46s	175	Firm staple, with spiral crimp, and corkscrew tip. Lustrous.	Medium-thick yarn. Quick and easy for beginners.	As above

CHARACTERISTICS OF NEW ZEALAND BREED WOOLS (Cont.)

Class	Breed	Micron	Qual. No.	Staple length (mm)	General characteristics	Notes on Spinning	Finished articles
Strong crossbred	Border Leicester	38–37	44s–46s	175	As above	As above	Floor rugs, wall hangings, upholstery.
	English Leicester	40–38	40s–44s	190	Heavy handling wool, with firm staples and pointed tip.	Thick yarn.	As above
	Lincoln	42–38	36s–40s	230	Very firm staples with spiral crimp. Yellowy in colour.	Thick yarn. If lightly spun and plied, the yarn may look similar to mohair.	As above
	Drysdale	41–38	30s–34s	310	Heavy, harsh wool, with an open fleece. Dull, medullated appearance.	Thick yarn, very coarse and hairy.	As above
Down	Southdown	26–21	58s–64s	50	Finest and softest of the high-bulk down wools. Spongy.	Not for beginners as short in staple. Thick-medium yarns, that are crease-resistant and spongy.	Lightweight knitted crocheted garments. Uncrushable woven fabrics.
	South Suffolk	31–28	52s–56s	75	Spongy wool, with no clear staple or crimp	As above	As above
	Suffolk	29–28	54s–56s	90	As above	As above	As above
	Hampshire	29–28	54s–56s	90	As above	As above	As above
	Dorset Down	29–26	54s–58s	75	As above	As above	As above
	Dorset Horn	33–28	50s–56s	100	As above	As above	As above
Cheviot	Cheviot	33–28	50s–56s	100	Harsh handling wool with a chalky colour. Spongy.	Not for beginners. Medium-thick yarn.	Blankets and knee Rugs. Knitted and crocheted garments.

SHEEP BREEDS OF GREAT BRITAIN

Breed	Quality No. or Count	Staple Length (mm)	Uses
Longwool breeds			
Border Leicester	40s–46s	150–255	
Cotswold	46s–48s	180–255	
Dartmoor	36s–40s	255–305	
Devon Longwool	32s–36s	305	
Kent/Romney	48s–56s	150–180	Knitting yarn, usually
Leicester	40s–46s	305–355	worsted spun.
Lincoln Longwool	38s–44s	305–405	
South Devon	36s–40s	180	
Teeswater	40s–48s	305	
Wensleydale	40s–48s	355	
Whiteface Dartmoor	32s–44s	255–305	
Shortwool breeds			
Clun Forest	56s–58s	76–100	
Devon Closewool	46s–50s	76–100	
Dorset Down	56s–58s	50–76	
Dorset Horn	54s–58s	76–100	
Hampshire Down	56s–58s	50–90	
Kerry Hill	56s–58s	100	
Llanwenog	56s–58s	76	
Oxford	50s–58s	150	
Radnor	50s–58s	76–180	Shawls, knitted garments,
Ryeland	56s–58s	76–100	blankets, knee rugs.
Shropshire	58s–58s	90–115	
Southdown	56s–60s	25–65	
Suffolk	54s–58s	50–76	
Orkney	50s–56s	40–76	
Shetland	56s–60s	100	
Soay	44s–50s	50–150	
Jacob	44s–56s	76–150	
Manx Loughton	44s–48s	76–130	
St Kilda	48s–50s	50–150	
Mountain/Hill breeds			
Cheviot	50s–56s	100	
Dalesbred	32s–40s	200	
Derbyshire Gritstone	50s–56s	150–200	
Exmoor Horn	50s–56s	76–100	
Herdwick	28s–32s	130	
Lonk	32s–44s	100–150	Carpets or outer garments
Rough Fell	32s–36s	200	
Scottish Blackface	28s–32s	200–330	
Swaledale	28s–32s	200–305	
Welsh Mountain	36s–50s	50–100	
Black Welsh Mountain	36s–50s	100	

SHEEP BREEDS OF GREAT BRITAIN (Cont.)

Breed	Quality No. or Count	Staple Length (mm)	Uses
Cross-breds			
Colebred	48s–54s	100–180	
Masham	44s–48s	150–180	
Romney/Kent Halfbred	56s–58s	50–100	Knitting yarns
Scottish Greyface	32s–48s	150–305	
Welsh Halfbred	48s–54s	130–150	

SHEEP BREEDS OF USA

Breed	Quality No. or Count	Staple Length (mm)
Fine wool breeds		
Rambouillet Merino	62s–70s	60–90
Delaine Merino	64s–80s	65–90
Medium Wool Breeds		
Southdown	56s–60s	50
Shropshire	48s–56s	65
Hampshire	48s–56s	50–65
Suffolk	48s–56s	50–65
Oxford	64s–50s	76–130
Dorset	48s–56s	76–100
Cheviot	48s–56s	76–100
Crossbred Wool Breeds		
Corriedale	50s–60s	100
Columbia	50s–60s	90–130
Montadale	—	—
Panama	50s–60s	—
Romeldale	58s–60s	—
Targhee	58s–60s	76

SHEEP BREEDS OF AUSTRALIA

These are similar to New Zealand breeds. Many strains of Merino have been bred in Australia, ranging in quality no. (count) from 50s–70s+. The name 'comeback' is unique to Australia, and is Merino crossed with a long-woolled breed, usually Lincoln, which has already been crossed with the Merino. Polwarth, Cormo, Zenith and Polmo are comeback breeds.

APPENDIX B:
ASHFORD WHEELS AND ACCESSORIES

ASHFORD TRADITIONAL WHEEL: SCOTCH TENSION

Specifications
Wheel diameter 560mm (22in)
Orifice 10mm (⅜in)
Bobbin capacity 100gm (3–4oz)
Drive ratio 6.6:1 and 10.5:1
Weight 8kg (17.5lb)

Optional accessories
Basic jumbo flyer unit
Complete jumbo flyer unit
Double drive flyer unit
Large pulley flyer
Flax distaff

This is the most popular wheel, and is suitable for all types of spinning. It will spin medium/fine to medium/bulky wool, using the two drive ratios, and the splayed-leg construction makes it stable for fast spinning. An upright lazy Kate is included.

ASHFORD TRADITIONAL DELUXE WHEEL: SCOTCH TENSION

Specifications
Wheel diameter 560mm (22in)
Orifice 15mm (⅝in)
Bobbin capacity 125gm (4–5oz)
Drive ratio 6.1:1 and 9:1
Weight 8kg (17.5lb)

Optional accessories
Double drive flyer unit
Basic jumbo flyer unit
Complete jumbo flyer unit
Flax Distaff

This wheel has a larger orifice for spinning bulky and textured yarns. It also has a greater bobbin capacity than the other Traditional wheels, making it a more suitable wheel for spinning medium/bulky yarn. An upright lazy Kate is included.

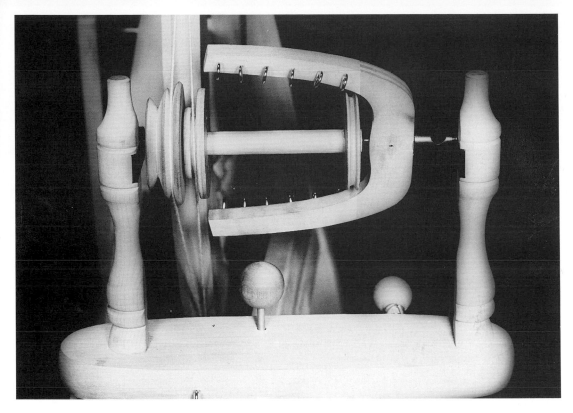

Detail of flyer

ASHFORD TRADITIONAL WHEEL: DOUBLE BELT

Specifications
Wheel diameter 560mm (22in)
Orifice 10mm (⅜in)
Bobbin capacity 100gm (3–4oz)
Drive ratio 8.5:1, 12.5:1 and 15:1
Weight 8kg (17.5lb)

Optional accessories
Complete jumbo flyer unit
Flax distaff

This wheel with the double belt system, also has the Scotch tension option attached, and it needs only a few seconds to convert from one to the other. To convert, place both drive belts on the spindle whorl, where they will form a single drive belt. The Scotch brake is unwound and taken over the bobbin whorl, and the spring is attached to the hook. For very fine spinning, place the doubled belt around the bobbin whorl, and the Scotch brake around the spindle whorl. This gives a ratio of 15:1. Many beginners start with the Scotch tension system, and then convert to the other when they become more proficient.

With a drive ratio of 8.5:1 on the larger spindle whorl, this wheel is capable of spinning finer wool than the previous Traditional wheel. For bulky spinning it would be best to add the complete jumbo flyer unit. An upright lazy Kate is included.

Detail of flyer

ASHFORD TRAVELLER WHEEL: SCOTCH TENSION

Specifications
Wheel diameter 460mm (18in)
Orifice 10mm (⅜in)
Bobbin capacity 100gms (3–4oz)
Drive ratio 5.2:1 and 8.9:1
Weight 7kg (15lb)

Optional accessories
Large pulley flyer
Basic jumbo flyer unit

This wheel is a type of castle wheel, as it has the flyer and bobbins above the wheel, not to one side, as with the Traditional wheels. It is a smaller wheel, and is suitable, as the name suggests, for travelling. It is also useful for spinners with little storage space at home. The lazy Kate is built in on the front of the wheel. Because the drive wheel is smaller than the other wheels, the spinner will treadle faster, but the connecting rod, from the treadle to the crankshaft, is short, and treadling requires little effort.

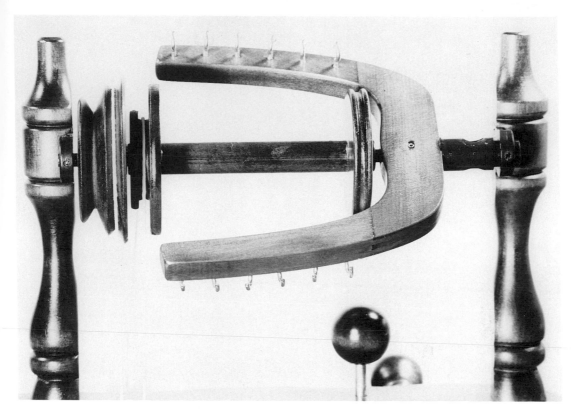

Detail of flyer

ASHFORD TRAVELLER WHEEL: DOUBLE BELT

Specifications
Wheel diameter 460mm (18in)
Orifice 10mm (⅜in)
Bobbin capacity 100gm (3–4oz)
Drive ratio 6.8:1, 10.1:1 and 12.3:1
Weight 7kg (15lb)
This is a double belt wheel that can be converted to the Scotch tension system, using the same method of conversion as with the Traditional double belt wheel. In other features, it is the same as the previous Traveller wheel, but is capable of spinning finer yarn because of the higher drive ratios.

Detail of Elizabeth Wheel:

A. Tension adjustment
B Scotch tension option
C Base board

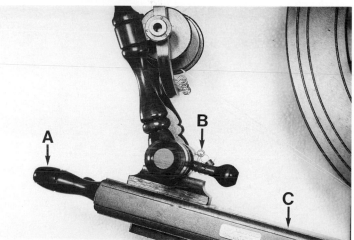

ELIZABETH WHEEL

Specifications
Wheel diameter 560mm (22in)
Orifice 10mm (⅜in)
Bobbin capacity 100gm (3–4oz)
Drive ratio 8.5:1, 12.5:1 and 15:1
Weight 9kg (20lb)

This is a more intricately turned, double belt wheel, particularly suitable for fine spinning, with drive ratios of 8.5:1 and 12.5:1. A Scotch tension system option is included, and the wheel can be converted, using the same method of conversion as with the Traditional double belt wheel. The Scotch tension system will give soft spinning and plying, while the double belt system will lend itself to firm-twist yarn. The lazy Kate is a horizontal type, which gives great stability when plying. The extra spokes add balance and weight to the wheel, which aids treadling.

To alter the double belt tension, turn the tension adjustment handle, noted in insert B. A ratio of 15:1 can be obtained by following the instructions on page 131.

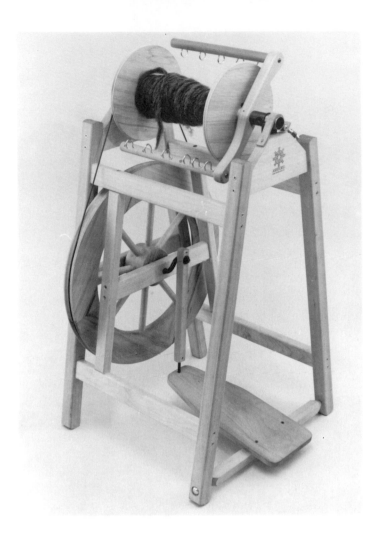

Wingnuts for adjusting flyer unit

ASHFORD COUNTRY SPINNER

Specifications
Wheel diameter 460mm (18in)
Orifice 23mm (⅞in)
Bobbin capacity 900gr–1kg (appx 34oz)
Drive ratio 3.8:1
Weight 6.5kg (14lb)
Height to orifice (720mm (28½in)

This is a redesigned Bulky Spinner, designed to spin extra bulky wool, as used in rug weaving or for bulky, knitted garments, hence the large orifice, bobbin capacity and appropriate drive ratio.

The wheel has a sensitive, leather, flyer-brake system and the bobbin is driven by a stretch drive-cord. The large wheel is weighted to start always in the correct position. The treadle board is large enough for two feet and heel-and-toe action.

Bulky yarn is spun in a different manner from fine or medium yarn, and instructions are given in Chapter Five.

ASHFORD SCHOLAR WHEEL

Specifications
Wheel diameter 460mm (18in)
Orifice 10mm (⅜in)
Bobbin capacity 225gm (8oz)
Drive ratio 5.4:1
Weight 5kg (11lb)
Height to orifice 715mm (28in)

This wheel is particularly suitable for students and beginners, with its easy-learning drive ratios, large wheel, Scotch tension system of flyer-drive bobbin-brake, stretchy drive cord and large treadle board for two feet and heel-and-toe action.

It has a folding treadle assembly for portability and storage. A Lazy Kate is conveniently built-in to take the two extra bobbins.

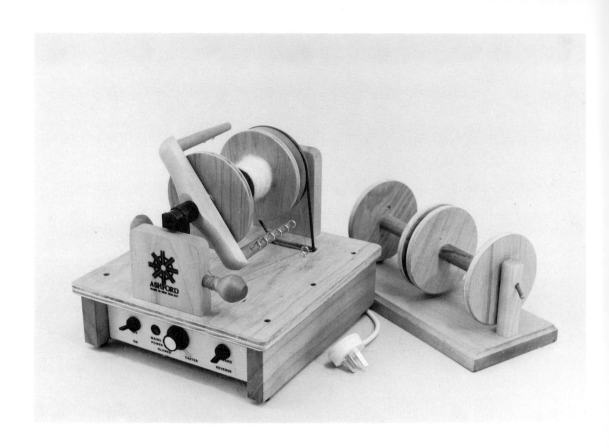

THE ASHFORD ELECTRONIC SPINNER

Specifications
Orifice 15mm (⅝in)
Bobbin capacity 225gm (8oz)
Weight 3.4kg (7½lb)
Voltage 90 watt, 220 volt
Size 280mm (11in) × 260mm (10in) × 190mm (7½in)

This electronic spinner incorporates the Scotch tension and has adjustable drive belt tension. The powerful 90 watt, 220 volt motor runs quietly and is fitted with suppressors to eliminate TV and radio interference.

There are three control switches. On the left is an on/off switch, with a red light to indicate when the machine is switched on. The centre control is the speed setting, and this can be adjusted from very slow to very fast, with a good variation of speeds to suit all spinners. This control is near your hands so that speed adjustments can be made while spinning. On the right is a reverse/forward control, one for spinning, one for plying.

This machine will suit spinners who have limited or no use of their legs. It is also suitable for those who have very little space, as it is compact and easy to carry. The large flyer and orifice allow for fine and bulky yarns. Three large jumbo bobbins and separate Lazy Kate are included.

ASHFORD ACCESSORIES

A. BASIC JUMBO FLYER UNIT
This unit consists of the jumbo flyer, 1 jumbo bobbin, and the front upright. It can be attached to the Traditional, Deluxe, and Traveller wheels.

B. COMPLETE JUMBO FLYER UNIT
This unit consists of the jumbo flyer, 4 jumbo bobbins, maiden bar, 2 uprights, knobs and adjusting board. It can be attached to the Traditional, Deluxe, and Traditional Double belt wheels.
Specifications
Orifice 15mm (⅝ in)
Bobbin capacity 225gm (8oz)
Drive ratio 4.3:1 and 9:1

DOUBLE BELT FLYER UNIT
This unit converts the Traditional and Deluxe wheels to the double belt system. It consists of the flyer and whorl, four bobbins, maiden bar, two uprights, knobs, and adjusting board.
Specifications
Orifice 10mm (⅜ in)
Bobbin capacity 100gm (3–4oz)
Drive ratio 8.5:1 and 12.5:1

FLAX DISTAFF (see photo **48**)
This can be attached to all three Traditional wheels for flax spinning. See Chapter Six for details on spinning flax.

ASHFORD SPINNING CHAIR
This is a traditional spinning chair. It has a tall, straight back which will support the spinner and lessen back strain while spinning. Adjust the seat to the correct height with a cushion. When standing next to the chair, the seat should come to just below your knee-cap.
Specifictions
Seat height 430mm (17in)
Overall height 960mm (38in)
Weight 4.8kg (10.5lb)

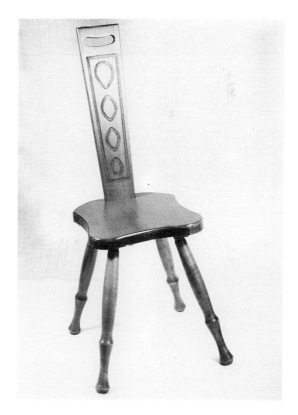

Ashford spinning chair

For a summary of Ashford wheels, see over.

Wheel	Ratio		Wheel Diameter	Orifice	Bobbin Capacity	Weight	Optional Accessories	Types of yarn. Comments
	Low	High						
Traditional	6.6:1	10.5:1	560mm (22in)	10mm (3/8in)	100gm (3–4oz)	8kg (17.5lb)	Basic Jumbo Flyer Unit Complete Jumbo Flyer Unit Double Drive Flyer Unit Flax Distaff Large pulley Flyer	Spins all types of yarns, from fine-bulky.
Traditional Double Drive	8.5:1	12.5:1	560mm (22in)	10m (3/8in)	100gm (3–4oz)	8kg (17.5lb)	Complete Jumbo Flyer Unit Flax Distaff	Spins finer wool than Traditional wheel.
Traditional Deluxe	6.1:1	9:1	560mm (22in)	15mm (5/8in)	125gm (4–5oz)	8kg (17.5lb)	Basic Jumbo Flyer Unit Complete Jumbo Flyer Unit Double Drive Flyer Unit Flax Distaff	Has larger orifice and greater bobbin capacity than other Traditional wheels
Traveller	5.2:1	8.9:1	460mm (18in)	10mm (3/8in)	100gm (3–4oz)	7kg (15lb)	Basic Jumbo Flyer Unit Large pulley flyer	Easy to carry and store
Traveller Double Drive	6.8:1	10.1:1	460mm (18in)	10mm (3/8in)	100gm (3–oz)	7kg (15lb)		Spins a finer yarn than Traveller
Elizabeth	8.5:1	12.5:1	560mm (22in)	10mm (3/8)	100gm (3–4oz)	9kg (20lb)		Particularly suitable for fine spinning
Country	3.5:1	–	460mm (18in)	23mm (7/8in)	965gm 34oz	6.5kg (14lb)		Spins bulky wool
Scholar	4.9:1	6.2:1	460mm (18in)	15mm (5/8in)	225gm (8oz)	5kg (11lb)		Spins medium-bulky wool. Easy to carry and store
Jumbo Flyer Unit (on Traditional wheel)	4.3:1	9:1	–	15mm (5/8in)	225gm (8oz)			
Jumbo Flyer Unit (on Traveller wheel)	3.5:1	7.4:1	–	15mm (5/8in)	225gm (8oz)			
Double Drive Flyer Unit (on Traditional & DeLuxe)	8.5:1	12.5:1	–	10mm (3/8in)	100gm (3–4oz)			
Electronic Spinner				15mm (5/8in)	225gm (8oz)	3.4kg 7.5lb		Volts – 220v 110v motor available

Walter Ashford, founder,
at his drawing board

A corner of Ashford's Museum

Turning spokes on the automatic lathe

Walter Ashford inspects wheels in production

APPENDIX C: ASHFORD DISTRIBUTORS

NEW ZEALAND

Ashford Handicrafts Ltd
P.O. Box 474
Ashburton
Tel: (053) 89087

AUSTRALIA

Ashford Handicrafts Ltd
Travellers Rest
Snowy Mountains Highway
Cooma NSW 2630
Tel: 008-026397

AUSTRIA

Alles Zum Gesunden Bauen and Wohnen
Ing Volkmar Baurecker
Hirrshgasse 22A
4020 Linz
Tel: (0732) 277285

BELGIUM

Artisans
Boulevard Paul Janson, 11–13
6000 Charleroi
Tel: (071) 316505

CANADA

Treenway Crafts Ltd
725 Caledonia
Victoria BC V8T 1B4
Tel: (604) 383-1661

DENMARK

Elsa Krogh
Havndalvej 40
9550 Mariager
Tel: (08) 542253

Spindegrej Struer
Venogade 3
DK 7600 Stuer
Tel: (07) 854944

FALKLAND ISLANDS

Spinning and Weaving Guide
P.O. Box 1255
Stanley

FINLAND

Toijalan Kaidetehdas KY
PL 25
37801 Toijala
Tel: (937) 21095

FRANCE

Celle Bernheim and fils
33 Rue de Jeuneurs
Paris
Tel: 233 45 95

WEST GERMANY

Fredrich Traub KG
D-7065 Winterbach
Schorndorfer Str Be 18
Tel: (07181) 77055

HONG KONG

Mr David Epstein
11th Floor Sincere Insurance Bldg
4–6 Hennessy Road, Wanchai
Tel: 5 290250

IRELAND

Craftspun Yarns Ltd
Johnstown–Naas
County Kildare
Tel: (045) 76881

JAPAN

Ananda Co Ltd
80 Jyomyo-ji
Kamakura City

Ocean Trading Co Ltd
8th Floor, 1–2
Kyoto Toshiba Bldg
25 Hira-machi, Saiin
Ukyo-ku, Kyoto
Tel: (075) 314 8720

Mariya Handicrafts Ltd
Kita-1, Nishi-3
Chuo-Ku, Sapporo 060
Tel: (011) 221 3307

JAPAN continued
Sanyo Trading Co
2F Hashimoto-kaikan
1-5, 1-Chome
Higashikanda, Chiyoda-Ku
Tokyo 101
Tel: 03-861-7321

REPUBLIC OF KOREA

Haelim Trade Co Ltd
C.P.O. Box 1653
Seoul
Tel: 752 8271

NETHERLANDS

Falkland Natuurgarens
Driebergen
Tel: 03438-18155

NORWAY

Spinningcr
Boks 36
1362 Billingstad

PAPUA NEW GUINEA

Eastern Highland Cultural Centre
c/o Mrs Anne Montgomery
P.O. Box 37
Kainantu

SAUDI ARABIA

Saudi Arts House
P.O. Box 1702
Riyadh

SINGAPORE

Hands DIY Superstore Pte Ltd
921 Bukit Timah Road 03-01
TCB Building
Tel: 4697455

SPAIN

Indigo Estudio Textil
Churruca
19-1. Est Izoda
Madrid 4

SWEDEN

Bellis Hemslojd
P.O. Box 4046
S.250-04 Helsingborg
Tel: (042) 298128

SWITZERLAND

Spinnstube
Sch miedengasse 6
2502 Biel
Tel: (032) 22 2960

Artesania
4953 Scharzenbach
b/Huttwil
Tel: (063) 721152

M Forter
Wiesenstr 5
9445 Rebstein
Tel: (71) 77 29 09

UNITED KINGDOM

Haldane & Company
Gateside
by Cupar
Fife KY14 7ST
Tel: (03376)-469

UNITED STATES

Crystal Palace Yarns
3006 San Pablo Avenue
Berkeley CA94702
Tel: (415) 548 9988

GLOSSARY

Break: Tender part of a staple, which will break under strain.

Carding: Breaking up a compact fibre mass to give it less density and make it more even.

Crimp: The wave pattern in a staple of wool.

Crossbred: A term generally applied to wool from long wool sheep breeds.

Drafting: The pulling out and reducing of fibres.

Fulling: Washing and finishing process for woollen cloth.

Lazy Kate: Bobbin holder for plying.

Medullated: A 'hollow' fibre, with a central core of medulla cells.

Micron: An abbreviated form of the word micrometre; one millionth of a metre.

Mordant: Chemical used in dyeing to fix the colour.

Niddy noddy: Apparatus used for winding yarn into skein form.

Orifice: Opening in the end of the spindle shaft, through which the spun yarn passes.

Plying: Spinning singles yarns together to form a plied yarn.

Rolag: Coil of carded wool.

Roving: A long, continuous arrangement of unspun fibre, immediately prior to the stage of worsted spinning.

Scouring: The process of removing the natural grease and dirt in wool.

Singles: One strand of yarn.

Sliver: A light, rope-like arrangement of carded wool fibres.

Spindle: A weighted shaft which imparts a twist to form a thread.

Strick: Length of prepared flax fibre.

Staple: A lock of fleece wool.

Top: A smooth, parallel arrangement of wool fibres after carding and combing.

Whorl: A pulley mounted on a spindle.

Yolk: A mixture of wax and sweat in wool.

BIBLIOGRAPHY

Anderson, Beryl *Creative Spinning, Weaving, and Dyeing*, Angus and Robertson, 1971.

Amos, Alden *Spinning Wheel Primer*, Straw Into Gold Editions, California, 1976.

Bains, Patricia *Spinning Wheels, Spinners and Spinning*, Batsford, London, 1977.

Cox, Truda *Beginning Spinning*, Wentworth Books, Australia, 1972.

Davenport, Elsie *Your Handspinning*, Sylvan Press, London, 1953.

Duncan, Molly *Creative Crafts with Wool and Flax*, A.H. & A.W. Reed, New Zealand, 1971.

Duncan, Molly *Spin Your Own Wool,* 2nd ed., A.H. & A.W. Reed, New Zealand, 1972.

Fannin, Allen *Handspinning: Art and Technique* Van Nostrand Reinhold Co, New York, 1970.

Grassett, K. *Complete Guide to Handspinning* Select Books (London School of Weaving).

Horne, Beverley *Fleece In Your Hands*, New Zealand Spinning, Weaving and Woolcrafts Society, 1974. (revised ed. Interweave Press, Colorado, 1979).

Jackson, C. & Plowman, J. *The New Zealand Woolcraft Book*, Collins, 1980.

Kluger, M. *The Joy of Spinning*, Simon and Schuster, New York, 1971.

Kroll, Carol *The Whole Craft of Spinning*, Dover Publications, New York, 1981.

Leadbeater, Eliza *Handspinning*, Select Books, 1976.

Milner, Ann *I Can Spin a Different Thread* John McIndoe, New Zealand 1980.

Ross, Mabel *The Essentials of Handspinning*, published by the author, 1980.

Ross, Mabel *The Essentials of Yarn Design For Handspinners*, published by the author, 1983.

Simmons, Paula *Spinning And Weaving With Wool*, Pacific Search Press, Seattle, 1977.

Simmons, Paula *Spinning For Softness And Speed*, Madrona Publishers Inc., Seattle, 1982.

Teal, Peter *Hand Woolcombing and Spinning*, A.H. & A.W. Reed, New Zealand, 1977.

Wickens, Hetty *Beginners Guide to Spinning*, Butterworth & Co. Ltd, United Kingdom, 1982.

Young, Joan *This is Wool*, NZ Wool Board, 1965.

New Zealand Sheep and Their Wool, NZ Wool Board, 1980.

Home Dyeing and Spinning by London Pride, Whitcombe & Tombs, N.Z.

Spinning, From the first ten years of 'Shuttle Spindle & Dyepot' 1979, Handweavers Guild of America, Inc.

Fibre Facts for Spinners and Weavers, published by Wellington Wool Festival Commiteee, 1982.

Spindles and Shafts, published by New Zealand Spinning, Weaving and Woolcrafts Society, 1980.

101 Questions For Spinners, Straw Into Gold Editions, California, 1978.

Dyeing

Lloyd, Joyce *Dyes From Plants of Australia and New Zealand*, A.H. & A.W. Reed, New Zealand, 1971.

Milner, Ann *Natural Wool Dyes and Recipes*, John McIndoe, New Zealand, 1971.

Thurstan, Violetta *The Use Of Vegetable Dyes*, Dryad Press, United Kingdom, 1968.

Felting
Marianna Ekert *Handmade Felt*, Textile Tools, New Zealand, 1984.

Knitting
The Woolgatherers' Handspun Pattern Book published by the Albury-Woodonga Handweavers & Spinners Guild, Australia.

INDEX